DEAR OCT

A Comedy in Th

by
DODIE SMITH

Samuel French – London
New York – Sydney – Toronto – Hollywood

DEAR OCTOPUS

Produced at the Queen's Theatre, Shaftesbury Avenue, London, on September 14th, 1938, with the following cast of characters:

CHARLES RANDOLPH	Leon Quartermaine.
DORA RANDOLPH	Marie Tempest.
HILDA RANDOLPH	Nan Munro.
MARGERY HARVEY	Madge Compton.
CYNTHIA RANDOLPH	Valerie Taylor.
NICHOLAS RANDOLPH	John Gielgud.
HUGH RANDOLPH	John Justin.
GWEN (FLOUNCY) HARVEY	Sylvia Hammond.
WILLIAM (BILL) HARVEY	Pat Sylvester.
KATHLEEN (SCRAP) KENTON	Muriel Pavlow.
BELLE SCHLESSINGER (their Sister-in-law)	Kate Cutler.
EDNA RANDOLPH (Hugh's Mother)	Una Venning.
LAUREL RANDOLPH (Hugh's Wife)	Jean Ormonde.
KENNETH HARVEY (Margery's Husband)	Felix Irwin.
GRACE FENNING (Dora's Companion)	Angela Baddeley.
NANNY PATCHING (a Nurse)	Annie Esmond.
GERTRUDE (a Parlourmaid)	Margaret Murray.

HILDA RANDOLPH, MARGERY HARVEY, CYNTHIA RANDOLPH, NICHOLAS RANDOLPH (their Children)

HUGH RANDOLPH, GWEN (FLOUNCY) HARVEY, WILLIAM (BILL) HARVEY, KATHLEEN (SCRAP) KENTON (their Grandchildren)

The Play produced by GLEN BYAM SHAW in conjunction with the Author.

SYNOPSIS OF SCENES

The action of the play takes place at the Randolphs' country house in North Essex, during a week-end in late autumn.

ACT I

The Hall. Friday evening.

ACT II

The Nursery. Saturday.

SCENE 1.—Morning.
SCENE 2.—Afternoon.
SCENE 3.—Late evening.

ACT III

The Dining-room. Sunday evening.

SCENE 1.—Before dinner.
SCENE 2.—After dinner.

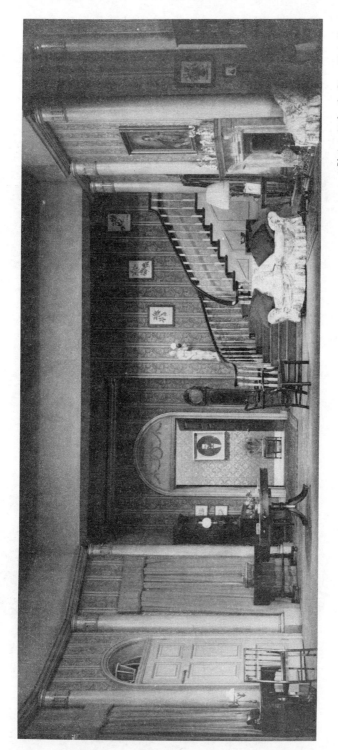

Act II, Scene 1

Act II, Scene 2

DEAR OCTOPUS

ACT I

SCENE.—*The hall of the Randolphs' country house in North Essex. The house was built in early Victorian days but on Georgian lines and, though much of the furniture is heavy and old-fashioned, the general atmosphere is pleasant and comfortable.*

On the R. are two tall sash-windows, with a door between them leading to the porch and front door. In the R. of the back wall are double doors leading to the dining-room, and on the L. of this wall a handsome staircase, at the bend of which is a plaster figure holding a lamp. In the upper part of the L. wall is an archway leading to a passage, and below this a large open fireplace, near which are a low-backed sofa, several chairs and a fender-stool. There is a round table R.C., a smaller one R. of the stairs, and various other pieces of furniture, including a grandfather clock. There are a good many pictures ; a painting of a young officer hangs over the fireplace.

(See Photograph of Scene.)

TIME.—*It is half-past nine on a Friday evening in late October.*

When the CURTAIN *rises the hall is empty. It is lit by the light from three paraffin lamps, turned very low, and the glow from the fire. The sound of laughter comes from the dining-room. Down the stairs comes* BILL HARVEY, *a nice-looking little boy of about ten, in a flannel dressing-gown. He goes to the fire and works the bellows. Voices in the dining-room are heard again.* BILL *continues with the bellows until the logs burn brightly. He then settles on the fender-stool, putting the bellows on the floor below the fender-stool.*

GRACE FENNING (FENNY) *enters through the front door* R. *She is a slender woman of twenty-nine, unobtrusively pretty, with a pleasant, unaffected manner. She wears old tweeds and is carrying a few chrysanthemums.*

BILL. Hello, Fenny. (*He rises and comes* C.)

FENNY. Hello, Bill. What a marvellous fire. (*She turns up the lamp on the desk, takes the waste-paper basket from under the desk, and puts it above the table* R.C. *She then takes the roses from a vase on the table.*) Oh dear, no more roses. I did hope these would last the week-end. (*She starts to arrange the chrysanthemums.*)

7

BILL. I like chrysanthemums. (*He takes a flower, smells it and puts it in the vase.*) People say they haven't a smell, but they have.

FENNY. They just smell of autumn. It's misty outside.

(*There is laughter again in the dining-room.*)

Goodness, what a time they're being over dinner. Was everything all right ?

BILL. Quite, I think. I got sent out at dessert.

FENNY. What for ?

BILL. For telling Grannie about me and bananas. (*Leaning over the table to* FENNY.) Did you know that if I eat a banana I'm sick at once ?

FENNY. I shouldn't eat them, then.

BILL. I don't. But I did think Grannie would be interested. I just happened to tell her because she was eating a banana.

FENNY. So out you went.

BILL. Yes. It's funny, isn't it ? Lots of children come in for dessert, but I go out for it.

(*Voices from the dining-room.*)

FENNY. I wish they'd hurry up. The maids'll never get done.

BILL. Gertrude's stumping about like anything. (*He puts the roses in the basket and takes out a golden telegram envelope.*) It's nice having golden envelopes for Golden Wedding telegrams. Though, of course, you could send them for funerals if you liked. (*He replaces the envelope and crosses and sits on the* R. *arm of the sofa.*)

FENNY. There—that'll have to do. Now what ought I to do next ? (*Walking to the armchair* C.) I wonder if the bedrooms are all right. (*She flops into the chair.*) Oh dear, I oughtn't to have sat down. Pull me up again.

BILL (*going to* FENNY *and kneeling by her*). You stay where you are a bit. You look jolly tired. Have a bit of choc ? (*He produces a bar from his dressing-gown pocket.*)

FENNY. I'd love a bit.

(*Voices from the dining-room.*)

BILL (*giving her a piece*). Why didn't you come to dinner ?

FENNY. On a night like this ? Do you know we've never had the house so full since I came here.

BILL. Do you like being Grannie's companion ?

FENNY. Very much indeed.

BILL (*rising—eating chocolate*). I wouldn't. I'd rather be a maid. Maids have nights out.

FENNY. I could have nights out if I wanted them. You'd better grow up and take me to the pictures.

BILL. I wouldn't mind at all. I think you're a very good sort of woman, Fenny.

FENNY. Thank you, Bill.

BILL. Have some more chocolate ?

FENNY. No, thank you. (*She rises and crosses to the fire and replaces the bellows.*)

(BILL *puts the chocolate back in his pocket.*)

I'll have some sandwiches when Cynthia and Great-aunt Belle arrive.

BILL (*turning to* FENNY *and kneeling up on the* L. *arm of the sofa*). I've never seen Great-aunt Belle. I bet she's a gorgonzola. Oh, hello !

(KATHLEEN KENTON (SCRAP) *has appeared on the stairs. She is a small, thin, rather peaky-looking child, about nine, with a very shy manner.* BILL *rises and goes up* C.)

FENNY. Feeling better, Scrap ? (*She sits on the sofa.*)

SCRAP. I wasn't ill—only just didn't want any dinner. (*To* BILL.) Hasn't Auntie Cynthia come yet ?

FENNY. Not yet—but the car's gone to meet her.

BILL. Why do you particularly want to see her ?

SCRAP (*coming down* C.). I just do.

BILL. But you've never met her.

SCRAP. Well, I want to meet her. Oh ! (*She sees the roses in the waste-paper basket.*)

FENNY. They're dead.

SCRAP. Not this one—not quite. (*She picks one out.*) Things oughtn't to die before they have to. (*She smells the rose.*)

FENNY. Did you see the cable from your father ?

SCRAP. Yes. I'd rather like to see it again.

BILL (*crossing to the table*). It's here. (*Reading.*) " Congratulations on your Golden Wedding. Love to Scrap. David Kenton."

(SCRAP *takes it.*)

FENNY. Would you like to have it ? (*She rises to* R. *corner of the sofa.*)

SCRAP. Wouldn't Grannie mind ?

FENNY. Of course not.

SCRAP. Then I think I would. Fancy it coming all the way from Singapore.

BILL. Not really, you know. They just write them at the post office.

SCRAP. I know that perfectly well ! (*She gives back the telegram.*) I don't think I'll have it, thank you. (*She crosses to the stairs.*)

FENNY. It's the thought that matters, you know. They don't do *that* at the post office.

SCRAP. But I can remember the thought without a bit of paper, I expect. (*She runs upstairs.*) I'd like to know when Aunt Cynthia comes.

(*She disappears.*)

FENNY. You are a blighter, Bill. (*She moves to the fire.*)

BILL. Well, she's so jolly soppy. (*He crosses to the sofa and sits on the* R. *arm.*)

FENNY. She's still missing her mother.

BILL. It's two solid years since Aunt Nora died. I believe she thinks Aunt Cynthia's going to be like her because they were twins. Is she ?

FENNY. Like Nora ? (*Looking at the photograph on the table* L. *of the sofa.*) Not in the least. Oh, poor Scrap.

BILL. Oh lawks, I suppose I'll have to be kind to her. I wish we didn't have any dead people in the family. It sort of spoils the party.

(NICHOLAS RANDOLPH *enters* R. *He is thirty-five, attractive, but not conventionally good-looking. He crosses and dumps his suitcase on the floor* L.C.)

Glory, glory—Uncle Nick.

NICHOLAS. Hello, Bill.

(BILL *runs to him and butts with his head.*)

Don't butt me in the stomach. Fenny, my dear—hard at it, I suppose ? (*He moves down* L.C. *to* FENNY, *takes off his hat, coat and scarf and gives them to* BILL, *who puts them on the armchair* C.)

FENNY. Things are a bit hectic. Where did you put the car ?

NICHOLAS. Round at the back. Where's everyone ?

FENNY. Still at dinner. Are you going in—oh, but don't, or they'll never come out.

NICHOLAS. I'm filthy, anyhow—didn't leave the office till after eight. We've just landed the contract for all the Gusto publicity.

BILL. What, the beastly sauce stuff ?

NICHOLAS. The sauce may be beastly, but the advertisements are grand. We're getting them out a new set of slogans. I say, did you hear my broadcast last week ? (*He sits on the* R. *arm of the sofa.*)

FENNY (*in front of the fire*). Every word. It was beautifully clear.

BILL. You spoke so jolly fast they had to have a two-minute interval after you.

NICHOLAS. They said I was a bit speedy.

(BILL *moves the suitcase to* R.C. *in front of the table, opens it and takes out a tweed coat.*)

But they've asked me to speak again—it's a debate really, on the Ethics of Publicity.—Here, what do you think you're doing ?

BILL (*busy unpacking* NICHOLAS'S *suitcase*).   Looking for my present.

NICHOLAS.   Present ?   It isn't Christmas.

BILL.   I bet there is one, though.   Is this it ?   (*He holds up a parcel.*)

NICHOLAS.   No, that's Flouncy's.

(BILL *takes out another parcel.*)

And that's for Scrap.   I say, what's Scrap like ?

BILL.   Pretty sickening.   We have to be very gentle with her.

NICHOLAS (*rising, going to the suitcase and kneeling*).   Here, look out, that's my dress-shirt.   There you are, you loathsome boy.   (*He unearths* BILL'S *present.*)   And that's for Fenny.

(*He hands a little box to* FENNY, *who crosses and takes it.*   BILL *rises.*)

FENNY.   Why should I get anything ?

NICHOLAS.   I just thought you'd like it.

FENNY (*who has opened the box*).   Thank you, Nicholas.   It's charming.

(FENNY *takes a flower-posy from the box and fastens it to her dress, putting the box on the table.*   BILL *is trying to undo his parcel.*)

NICHOLAS.   This is mother's Golden Wedding present, and these are for Father.   (*He opens a jeweller's case, and also shows three old leather-bound books.*)

(FENNY *has knelt* L. *of the suitcase.*)

FENNY.   You are a generous person.

NICHOLAS (*patting her hand*).   Nonsense.   My dear, your hands are rough.   Have you been doing a lot of dirty work ?

FENNY.   Oh, odds and ends.   We've been a bit rushed. (*She rises and goes* L.C.)

NICHOLAS.   I must buy you some nice smelly glycerine and what-not.   We advertise some stuff called " Lily Hands," but it's really rather lousy.

BILL.   I'm not allowed to say lousy.   (*He gets his parcel undone.*)

NICHOLAS.   I am.   It just shows how unfair life is.   (*He puts the present back in the suitcase ; closes it and rises.*)

BILL (*dropping paper and string on the floor.*)   A paint-box—— Oh, you heavenly man !

(GERTRUDE, *the parlourmaid, a heavily-built woman of fifty, enters from the passage* L.)

NICHOLAS (*shaking hands with* GERTRUDE, C.). Good evening, Gertrude. How are you ?

GERTRUDE. Good evening, sir. (*To* FENNY.) Can't you get them out of the dining-room, miss ?

FENNY. Try not to upset yourself, Gertrude. I'll help you with the washing-up.

GERTRUDE. No, you won't, miss—you must be dog-tired yourself. You can't do it, Mr. Nicholas—turning two in family into fourteen in family with only a couple of girls from the village to help—and they haven't got enough sense to pick up the things they drop.

NICHOLAS (*looking into her face*.) Gertrude, you're not your sunny self.

GERTRUDE. No, I'm not, sir. And if we feel like this now, how are we going to feel by Monday ? You should just see cook's varicose veins.

BILL. *I've* seen them, haven't I, Gertrude ?

GERTRUDE. And a dance to-morrow, if you please—thirty people coming——

FENNY. She's been so splendid. It's just this sitting late over dinner.

NICHOLAS (*stepping up* R.). Here, I'll rout them out.

FENNY. No—leave it to me. Run along and wash.

NICHOLAS (*patting* GERTRUDE). Cheer up, Gertrude—think how slim you'll get.

(BILL *lifts the suitcase.*)

Drop that ; you'll strain yourself. (*He takes it from* BILL.)

BILL (*following him upstairs*). Your fire's all right, I had a look.

(*They disappear upstairs,* BILL *taking the paint-box.*)

GERTRUDE. Fires in every room.

FENNY (*crossing and collecting paper and string and putting it in the basket*). I know they're a curse. But the house is so cold and damp. *I* laid most of the fires.

GERTRUDE. You work your fingers to the bone, miss. It's a shame the way the mistress puts on you.

FENNY (*firmly*). Oh no, she doesn't. She's a perfect lamb and so's Mr. Randolph. You wouldn't let anyone else speak badly of them. (*She picks up the basket.*)

GERTRUDE. That's true enough, miss. (*She crosses to* FENNY.) There now, you've made me feel ashamed of myself.

FENNY. Nonsense, Gertrude—you're our tower of strength. [*She puts her arm round her.*) I'm sure we both want everything to be lovely this week-end. (*She crosses and puts the basket under the desk, then moves back to tidy the telegrams on the table.*)

GERTRUDE. Yes, of course, miss. They've been looking forward to it so—every living child under their roof and Miss Cynthia hasn't been home for seven years. I always say Golden Weddings are very beautiful—

(*Voices from the dining-room.*)

—only they did ought to come out of that dining-room.

FENNY. Wait—they're coming now. Round you go and I'll be along in a minute to help.

(*She goes up* R. *to turn up the lamp on the bookcase, then down to the table to collect the box which held the posy.* GERTRUDE *picks up* NICHOLAS'S *coat, etc., from the armchair* O. *and goes* L. *behind the sofa.*)

And, Gertrude, have you got any hand lotion ? (*She rubs her hand.*)

GERTRUDE. That's washing the nursery paint this morning. I've some Cream of Lotus Buds ; I'll lend you some. (*She hurries off* L.) Annie—they're coming out——

(FENNY *hurriedly turns up the lamp* L. *of the sofa.* CHARLES, DORA, HILDA, MARGERY, KENNETH, FLOUNCY, EDNA, HUGH *and* LAUREL *enter from the dining-room amid general conversation. The order of entrance is as follows :* KENNETH *and* HUGH *open the doors.* 1. DORA, *down to* R. *arm of the sofa.* 2. EDNA, *down to* O. 3. HILDA *and* LAUREL, *arm in arm with* CHARLES. 4. MARGERY *and* FLOUNCY, *to armchair* O. 5. KENNETH *and* HUGH, *after closing the doors. Both are smoking.* KENNETH *goes to behind the sofa,* HUGH *and* LAUREL *to the table* R.O. *and* HILDA *to the desk* R.)

DORA (*seventy-two, a small, white-haired and still pretty woman, charmingly dressed*). We're terribly late, Fenny. Is Gertrude ruffled ?

FENNY. It's quite all right, Mrs. Randolph. I'm just going to give her a hand.

(FENNY *goes into the dining-room.*)

DORA. Thank you, dear. Shall we sit here or in the drawing-room ?

EDNA (*forty-five, handsome and very smart*). There's a splendid fire here, Mrs. Randolph. (*She crosses to it, shivering.*)

DORA. Very well, dear—just tidy the hearth, will you ? (*She sits on the sofa.*)

CHARLES (*seventy-five, a very handsome old man*). We shall need some more chairs. (*He remains standing up* O.)

LAUREL (*twenty-two, a very lovely, fair girl*). Can we get some from the drawing-room for you, Mr. Randolph ?

CHARLES. Thank you, Laurel. Let me see now——

(EDNA *sits on the fender-stool and sweeps the hearth.*)

MARGERY (*forty, fair, pretty, but much too fat*). Don't count Flouncy, because she's going to bed. (*She sits in the armchair* C.)

FLOUNCY (*twelve, golden-curled, plump and affected*). Oh, Mummie, I can't. I'm terribly full. (*She sits on the arm of her mother's chair.*)

DORA. The child's quite right, Margery—she oughtn't to sleep on top of that heavy meal. She'd better go for a brisk walk round the garden.

FLOUNCY. I don't want to go for a brisk walk. I just want to sit still.

DORA. Sitting still won't digest your dinner. Run along, now. You go with her, Hilda.

HILDA (*forty-two, plain, intelligent and rather nervy*). I've got to telephone, Mother. (*She has been making notes at the desk.*)

(EDNA *rises from the fender-stool and sits in the chair down* L. *She takes a cigarette from her bag and lights it.*)

DORA. Who to, dear ?

HILDA. My secretary.

DORA. Write her a postcard, dear—the telephone's so expensive.

HILDA. I'll pay for the calls myself, Mother dear. It's an extremely important business matter. (*She returns to her notes.*)

KENNETH (*forty-five, pleasant-looking and stoutish*). I'll take you, Flouncy. I can do with a bit of exercise. (*He is behind the sofa.*)

DORA. Go with your father, dear.

(FLOUNCY *rises to between the chair and the sofa.*)

MARGERY. Your coat's in the cloakroom.

DORA. And put your goloshes on.

FLOUNCY. I don't have goloshes.

DORA. Then borrow mine. You'll find them in the boot-rack.

FLOUNCY. I don't like goloshes, Grannie. They make your feet look awful.

DORA. Your father won't mind how your feet look.

KENNETH (*at the arch* L.). Come along, Queen of Sheba.

(*He takes her through the archway* L.)

DORA. That child's getting conceited.

LAUREL (*looking up from the telegrams which she is examining with* HUGH). She'll grow out of it. I was terribly conceited at her age.

HUGH (*twenty-three, very nice-looking*). And still are, ugly.

CHARLES (*coming down to the table*). It's a pity you two are so plain. It doesn't give that baby of yours much chance in life.

HUGH. We're so terribly chocolate-boxy. We're hoping the baby'll inherit Mother's classic features.

DORA. How do you like being a grandmother, Edna ?

EDNA. I find it comparatively painless, thank you, Mrs. Randolph.

DORA. Nanny and I think the baby's got a look of Peter.

HUGH. Of Father ? I wish I could remember him.

MARGERY (*looking up at the painting over the mantelpiece*). Funny to think Peter would have been a grandfather.

(DORA *suddenly dabs her eyes with a handkerchief*.)

Why, Mother dear——

(CHARLES *quickly crosses to her*.)

DORA. It's nothing, dear. I was just wishing he could be here—and Nora, too. I'm quite all right now.

(KENNETH *and* FLOUNCY *return ready for their walk*. FLOUNCY *crosses to* R. *of the armchair* C.)

Have you got your goloshes on ?

FLOUNCY (*stopping and turning to* DORA). Yes, Granny.

DORA. They're such splendid things—I shall send you a pair. Now, walk briskly.

MARGERY. Don't keep her out too long, Ken.

KENNETH. We're just going to have a quick one at the " Green Man."

(*They go out* R.)

DORA. Surely he didn't mean that ?

MARGERY. Of course not, Mother dear.

DORA. I'm afraid his sense of humour isn't quite like ours. Perhaps it's living in Birmingham.

MARGERY. We don't live in Birmingham. We live right outside—practically in the country.

DORA. Still, it's not quite the same, is it, dear ?

(HILDA *crosses to* R. *of the sofa*.)

CHARLES. Now what about those chairs——

DORA. Sit down, Hilda.

HILDA. I've got to telephone, Mother.

DORA. Then telephone, dear, and get it over. You'll find it **very** draughty.

HILDA. Don't I know it.

DORA. And don't go on talking after the pip pip pip—

(HILDA *goes off* L.)

—because they charge you at once. Hilda's business can't be very well run if it won't take care of itself for a week-end.

(CHARLES *goes up to the round table* R. *of the stairs and picks up two books. He places one in the bookshelves up* R., *then sits in the chair below the shelves and reads the other.*)

HUGH. She's quite a big pot really, Grannie. I read an article on her the other day in a Pioneer Woman series.

LAUREL. What does she do ?

HUGH. She's an Estate Agent. She's put through one or two pretty big deals in house property.

DORA. It's a surprise to me that Hilda knows the back of a house from the front. (*She looks at her watch.*) After ten. (*Calling.*) Fenny.

(FENNY *comes to the dining-room door.*)

FENNY. Yes, Mrs. Randolph ?

DORA. Have the Tupkins girls gone back to the village yet ?

FENNY. No, Mrs. Randolph ; they're still here.

DORA. I promised their mother—Hugh—

(HUGH *comes below the table to* C.)

—I wonder if you'd run them back in your car ?   It's such a long, dark road and they really aren't quite right in the head—tell them to get ready, Fenny.

FENNY. Yes, Mrs. Randolph.

(FENNY *goes back into the dining-room.*)

HUGH. Is their name really Tupkins, Grannie ?

DORA. Yes, dear—at least, it's their mother's name—I'm afraid they're illegitimate twins.

HUGH (*enchanted*). Really, Grannie ?

DORA. Well, dear, villages are like that—we've been a little better since we had the cinema.

HUGE (*to* LAUREL, *as he crosses to the front door*). Coming ?

LAUREL. Righto. I'll get the coats while you start the car.

(*She runs off* L. HUGH *goes off* R.)

DORA. Edna dear, I wonder if you'd mind having one last look round the bedroom fires—

(EDNA *rises.*)

—particularly Aunt Belle's. I'm afraid she'll be very tired after **her** journey.

(EDNA *crosses above the sofa to* c.)

Take the coal-glove, dear, then you won't spoil your hands.

(EDNA *returns for it, then goes up.* LAUREL *comes back with the coats and runs into* EDNA.)

LAUREL.　Sorry.

(EDNA *exits up the stairs.*)

DORA.　Tell Hugh to drive very slowly, particularly by the gates, because the lodge cat generally sleeps in the middle of the drive—

(LAUREL *pauses below the table* R.C.)

—and be sure to take the girls right to their door and see their mother *gets* them.

LAUREL.　We will, Mrs. Randolph.

(*She goes off* R.)

DORA (*to* MARGERY).　Margery dear, just run along to the kitchen and see if you can do anything.　It's really time the sandwiches came in.

MARGERY (*rising*).　Very well, Mother dear.

(*She goes behind the sofa.* CHARLES *rises and puts his book in the shelves.*)

DORA.　And just see if Hilda's still telephoning.　I don't think she really understands about the pip pip pip.　(*Calling.*) Tell her it's elevenpence every time it pips.

(MARGERY *exits* L.)

(*To* CHARLES.)　Were you saying something about chairs ?

CHARLES (*crossing to* R. *arm of the sofa*).　I was, my love, but as you've successfully found little jobs for everyone, we've really far more chairs than we need.

DORA.　So we have.　Well, I shall be glad of a little breathing-space before the others arrive.　Oh, I do hope everything goes off well.　All our children lead such busy lives.　I should like this week-end to be a real *rest* for them.

CHARLES.　Yes, dear.　Is there anything you'd like me to do before I sit down ?

DORA.　I don't think so, dear.

(CHARLES *sits in the armchair* C.)

Just put another log on, will you ?

(CHARLES *rises and does so.*)

Charles——

CHARLES.　Yes, my love ?

(DORA *pats the sofa beside her.*)

DORA. I can't help feeling we ought to have gone to meet Cynthia.

CHARLES (*sitting on the sofa*). Now, you know we decided——

DORA. But were we right ? Oh, I agree we mustn't appear to be rushing at her, but—just the car and the chauffeur, it's so cold, so unwelcoming after seven years. If only I knew the reason——

CHARLES. Haven't we agreed to accept the reason she's given ? She's been busy, it hasn't been convenient—— After all, Paris is a long way.

DORA. Stuff and nonsense ! I'd have popped over to see her long ago if I hadn't been frightened of what I should find. Is that the car ?

CHARLES. No. Now, don't let yourself get jumpy. Sit back and relax. You know, I'm really very much touched that Belle should want to come down to us this week-end.

DORA. I daresay she's very glad to. She's probably pretty much at a loose end in England.

CHARLES. I can't imagine Belle at a loose end anywhere.

DORA. You must be prepared for a pretty big change in her.

CHARLES. I suppose so. Twenty-five years in America——

DORA. Twenty-five years anywhere. Charles, how old *is* Belle ?

CHARLES. I'm blessed if I know.

DORA. Now let's see. She married your brother William in eighty-nine. I'm sure she's older than I am.

CHARLES (*slowly*). She must be seventy-one.

DORA. I think she's older.

CHARLES. How strange.

DORA. What ?

CHARLES. To think of Belle as old. All that red-gold hair——

DORA. That'll be gone, anyhow. I wonder if she'll be white or just streaky. So many women go streaky. (*She pats her pretty white hair.*) I expect we shall get a bit of a shock.

CHARLES. What at ?

DORA. Her looks. After all, we've both kept pretty young.

CHARLES. You certainly have.

DORA. Well, I always had a good skin. That helps more than anything. I was thinking only to-day how much younger we seem than my parents at their Golden Wedding. Poor dears, they really were quite doddering. I've no intention of doddering if I live to be a hundred.

CHARLES. Quite right. Doddering's a mental attitude.

DORA. I don't think Belle will have worn well. Poor Belle, she'd never have taken William if she could have got you.

CHARLES. Nonsense. (*But he smiles reminiscently.*) I wonder what her American husband was like ?

(*A car is heard off* R.)

DORA. He certainly left her very well off. That *is* the car.

CHARLES (*rising*). Now keep calm, dear. (*He goes to the window.*) Yes, just coming up the drive. (*He looks again, then turns to her.*) Now, Dora dear, don't excite yourself. It's only Belle. Cynthia isn't there.

DORA (*rising up instantly*). Oh, Charles——!

CHARLES (*crossing up* C.). Now, my dear, there are two more trains to-night.

DORA (*taking a step down stage*). She's not coming. She'll never come.

CHARLES. Now quietly, dear. Belle's just here.

(CHARLES *crosses and opens the front door.*)

DORA. Belle, my dear——

(BELLE SCHLESSINGER *enters, a small, trim woman, very fashionably dressed. At first glance one would say she was twenty years younger than* DORA, *but it is an artificially preserved youth*).

BELLE. Isn't this splendid ! (*She kisses* CHARLES, *then crosses to* DORA.)

CHARLES (*at the front door*). Take the luggage up the back way.

VOICE OFF. Yes, sir.

(CHARLES *closes the door.*)

BELLE. Dora, you're as pretty as ever.

(*They kiss.*)

Well now, isn't this just too exciting !

CHARLES (*crossing after* BELLE). Let me take your coat.

(BELLE *slips out of her fur coat, pulls off her hat and gives them both to him. Her hair is golden-red, dyed, but very skilfully.*)

DORA (*gasping*). Belle !

BELLE. Have I changed so much ?

CHARLES. You haven't changed at all.

BELLE. If that isn't the nicest thing I've heard since I landed. (*She arranges herself at her bag-mirror.*) I can look better than this.

DORA. But it hasn't gone grey at all.

BELLE. It may be sea-green for all I know. It's a good twenty years since I saw its natural colour.

DORA. Do you mean it's dyed ?

BELLE. Well, it's *helped* Now, don't go looking at me

through a microscope, because I can't stand up to it. You want to get a quick general impression.

(BELLE *puts her gloves on the armchair* o., *sits and powders.* CHARLES *goes up and puts her hat and coat on the banisters.*)

Mind you, I wouldn't go to all this trouble if I could have grown old like you, Dora. You always were the prettiest creature.

CHARLES (*coming down to* DORA). My dearest Belle, you've defeated age.

DORA. It's extraordinary. We were just saying—— How old are you, Belle ?

BELLE. You don't know ? Then nobody knows—not one soul in the world. Isn't that fine ?

DORA. Aren't you going to tell us ?

BELLE. I am not. I never did believe in telling my age. And it won't be any use looking on my coffin, because it won't be on that.

DORA. Just as you wish, of course—but it seems a bit silly when one gets to our time of life.

BELLE. Dora, my mother used to talk like that when she was forty. It's all a question of one's attitude to life. I don't like old age. I don't like anything *about* old age and I'm not giving it any sort of helping hand. (*She finishes tidying up.*) There ! Now let's have a look at you two. Oh, you good-looking couple.

(CHARLES *puts* DORA *on the sofa and stands in front of the fire.*)

My, it's fun to be back in this room. I don't believe you've changed a thing.

DORA. We've had new cretonnes—at least three times.

BELLE. They've got the same sort of feel. Where am I sleeping ?

DORA. In Little Spare. You always liked that.

BELLE. Is Moses still in the bulrushes ?

DORA. Certainly. It's a very fine engraving.

BELLE. I slept there the first time I came here—when Will and I were engaged. (*To* CHARLES.) That must be—no, never add up years.

(BILL *comes downstairs.*)

Hello, who's here ?

BILL (*shaking hands*). I'm Bill.

DORA. Margery's youngest.

BILL. She knows. She sends us presents every Christmas. That was a very nice book you sent Flouncy last year. I expect I'm a bit older than you imagined.

BELLE. You certainly are.

BILL. She sent me a woolly rabbit.

BELLE. I do apologize.

BILL.   It's quite all right.   The dog liked it.

BELLE.   I suppose you're at school ?

BILL.   Not just at present.   I was expelled.

BELLE.   Whatever for ?

BILL.   For using bad language.   Would you like to know what I said ?

BELLE.   I certainly would.   We'll make a date for to-morrow.

DORA.   Now don't encourage him.

CHARLES.   It was only a silly little dame school.   He didn't say anything very bad.

BILL.   I said all I knew.

DORA.   Go to bed.

BILL (*leaning on the* R. *arm of the sofa*).   Hasn't Aunt Cynthia come ?

DORA.   Not yet, dear.   Belle, you're sure Cynthia wasn't on the platform ?

BELLE.   I was the one soul that got out of the train.

DORA.   I do hope nothing has gone wrong.

BELLE.   But surely she'd have called you up ?

BILL.   Called us up ?

(BILL *and* DORA *look at each other.*)

CHARLES.   That's American, Belle.

BELLE.   I know.   It's a catching language.   Rung you up, rung you up.   I'll cure myself in time.

(CYNTHIA *enters through the front door.   She is thirty-seven, with a sensitive, attractive, but faintly tragic face.   She is dressed in a black suit, simple but obviously from a famous model-house.   She is quite cheerful, but there is no colour or warmth in her manner.*)

CYNTHIA.   Hello, everybody.   (*She crosses in front of the table to* DORA.)

CHARLES.   Cynthia !

DORA (*rising*).   Oh, my dear—my dear, dear Cynthia.

CYNTHIA (*kissing her*).   Mother darling.   Father dear.   (*She kisses him.*)   Goodness, is it Aunt Belle ?

(*They shake hands.*)

(BILL *walks to behind* BELLE'S *chair, looking at* CYNTHIA.)

CHARLES.   How did you get here ?

CYNTHIA.   By the bus.   My suitcase is down at the " Green Man."

DORA (*to* BILL).   Tell Thompson to go for it at once.

BILL.   Righto, Grannie.   (*To* CYNTHIA.)   I'm Bill, I'll be back.

(*He goes off* L.)

CYNTHIA. He's grown up on me. He was crawling round the nursery last time I saw him.

CHARLES. I can't think why you wanted to come on the bus. It takes three hours.

CYNTHIA (*taking off her gloves*). I thought I'd like to drive through the villages. Things haven't changed much. Except for those hideous bungalows.

CHARLES. And the council houses. Still, this part's pretty unspoilt.

CYNTHIA. No electric light yet ?

DORA. It's coming to the village next year. But we shan't have it. I never did fancy having the house wired. (*To* CHARLES.) Just turn that lamp down, it's smoking.

(DORA *indicates the standard lamp and sits* C. *on the sofa.* CHARLES *does it.*)

Sit down, dear. (*She pats the sofa beside her.*) You must be stiff after that jolting bus.

CYNTHIA. I've walked it off. (*She sits.*)

DORA. My dear, you're not in mourning ?

CYNTHIA. Heavens, no, Mother. Everyone wears black in Paris.

BELLE. That looks remarkably like Raquelle.

CYNTHIA. It is. I work for her.

BELLE. As a mannequin ?

CYNTHIA (*undoing her coat*). Nothing so youthful and glamorous. Just a sort of receptionist and general odd-jobber. (*To* DORA.) The blouse is less funereal.

DORA. You're looking thin, my darling.

CYNTHIA. Thank God for that. I used to be terribly buxom. You two haven't changed a bit.

DORA. I'm afraid we have. It's seven years——

CYNTHIA. Yes. (*She rises abruptly, then slowly walks round the room to below the table* R.C.) This room's shrunk. I suppose rooms always do. Where's Fenny ? Where's everyone ?

DORA. They're about somewhere.

(BILL *and* SCRAP *appear on the stairs :* SCRAP *comes down* C. *to* CYNTHIA ; BILL *stands above the table.*)

CYNTHIA. Hello.

BILL. This is Scrap, Aunt Cynthia. She particularly wanted to see you.

DORA (*to* BELLE). Poor Nora's child.

CYNTHIA. This is our very first meeting, isn't it ?

SCRAP. Yes. (*She looks closely at* CYNTHIA. *The eagerness fades from her face, but she holds out her hand politely.*) How do you do ? I hope you had a pleasant journey.

DORA. And here's your Great-aunt Belle. Such a lot of new relations.

Bᴇʟʟᴇ (*shaking hands*). I always thought your name was Kathleen.

Sᴄʀᴀᴘ. It is, but Mummie always—I've always been called Scrap. (*She crosses to the* ʀ. *arm of the sofa.*) Grannie, would it be all right if I went to bed now ?

Dᴏʀᴀ. You ought to be in bed already. Run along. I'll look in when I come up.

Sᴄʀᴀᴘ. I expect I'll be asleep. (*She gives a little jerky bow to the company.*) Good night. (*She runs upstairs.*)

Cʜᴀʀʟᴇs. Good night, Scrap.

(Sᴄʀᴀᴘ *disappears.*)

Cʏɴᴛʜɪᴀ (*moving up to* Bɪʟʟ). I didn't exactly make a hit.

Bɪʟʟ. I think she was expecting you to be like her mother.

Cʏɴᴛʜɪᴀ. Like Norah ? Oh, poor little devil.

Dᴏʀᴀ. I'm very worried about her. I don't at all like the sound of this school she's at. I must write to her father. Bill, go to bed.

Bɪʟʟ (*crossing to* Dᴏʀᴀ). All right, Grannie, but it's no good. The house is so restless.

Bᴇʟʟᴇ (*rising*). Why don't you show me my room——

(Dᴏʀᴀ *rises.*)

No, sit down, Dora. (*To* Bɪʟʟ.) Maybe we'll find some candies.

(Bᴇʟʟᴇ *and* Bɪʟʟ *exit up the stairs.*)

Cʏɴᴛʜɪᴀ. I think I'll go up too, Mother. I want a wash. No, don't come, dear. Am I in my own room ?

Dᴏʀᴀ. Of course, my darling. Don't be long.

(Cʏɴᴛʜɪᴀ *goes up.* Dᴏʀᴀ *comes to the foot of the stairs.*)

Sandwiches are coming in later. (*She waits till* Cʏɴᴛʜɪᴀ *is out of sight, then speaks quietly.*) Charles, I knew it. There *is* something wrong with Cynthia—that hard, cold manner—— (*She comes back to the sofa and sits.*)

Cʜᴀʀʟᴇs (*moving up to* Dᴏʀᴀ). Now, Dora——

Dᴏʀᴀ. We've let it go too long. We've lost her, Charles.

Cʜᴀʀʟᴇs. Do try to keep calm, Dora. Our one chance of making contact is to be absolutely natural and casual. (*He sits beside* Dᴏʀᴀ.)

Dᴏʀᴀ. How can I be casual when I've only got one week-end ? My poor Cynthia. Anyone can see she's not happy.

Cʜᴀʀʟᴇs. There—my dear—I know how you feel. She was always your favourite.

Dᴏʀᴀ. I never had any favourites. I loved them all equally. But I always *liked* Cynthia best. We were such friends.

CHARLES. I wish the whisky would come in.
DORA. It's coming. Don't fuss.

(NICHOLAS *comes downstairs.*)

NICHOLAS. Hello.
CHARLES. Ah! Nicholas. (*He rises and stands in front of the fire.*)
DORA. Nicholas, my dear boy—why did no one tell me you were here?
NICHOLAS. Hello, Mother darling. (*He kisses her.*) How are you, Father?
CHARLES (*shaking hands*). Glad to see you, my boy.
NICHOLAS. Happy Golden Wedding. The real anniversary's on Sunday, isn't it?
DORA. Just see if Fenny's getting the sandwiches, will you, dear.
NICHOLAS. Right. I'll give her a hand.

(*He goes off* L. CHARLES *crosses and picks up* BELLE'S *gloves from the armchair* C.)

DORA. What did you think of Belle?
CHARLES. Astonishing. Not a day older.
DORA. Pouf! One soon sees.
CHARLES. I can't say I did. Of course, she always had a magnificent complexion.
DORA. She never had a complexion at all, she just had a skin. And I shouldn't think she's seen that for years.
CHARLES. Dora, really! (*He glances upstairs, then puts the gloves on the table* R.C. *and crosses back to* DORA.)
DORA. Oh, it's all right, she won't be down yet. And anyhow, she wouldn't mind. I must say she's always been very honest about her make-up. Dear me, it must be very worrying to take a face like that out in the rain.
CHARLES (*chuckling*). I do love you when you're being catty.
DORA. I'm not being catty at all. I think she's in a magnificent state of preservation. By the way, I've worked it out. She's seventy-three.
CHARLES. Nonsense. She's still in the sixties.
DORA. Now you're being simple. She's seventy-three at least, and I'm not at all sure she couldn't be seventy-five. I shall wear my silver to-morrow, not my black.
CHARLES. Whatever you wear, you'll cut her out. (*He is behind the sofa and puts his hand on her shoulder.*)
DORA (*catching his hand and looking up*). I *was* being catty.
CHARLES. You were, my love, you were. (*He kisses her on the top of the head.*)

(NICHOLAS *comes in from the* L. *with a tray of sandwiches. He crosses* C. *and rests the tray on the back of the armchair.*)

NICHOLAS. You two been having words ?

DORA. Certainly not.

NICHOLAS. I don't believe you. During my entire life the slightest disagreement between you has been settled by Father kissing you on the top of the head.

CHARLES. I sometimes kiss your mother on the top of the head when we have *not* had a disagreement.

NICHOLAS. One way and another it's remarkable she has a hair left. Sandwiches on this table ? (*He puts the tray on the table* R.C.)

DORA. That's right, dear, and bring up some chairs.

(CHARLES *gets the chair from up* R. NICHOLAS *meets him half-way and takes it from him to the table.* FENNY *has come in with a tray of cocoa. She comes down to the fire.*)

Yes, Fenny dear, put that on the stool. Cynthia loves cocoa.

(FENNY *puts the tray on the fender-stool and pours herself a cup.* MARGERY *has come in with the whisky-tray.*)

And the whisky on the table there.

(MARGERY *puts the tray on the round table* R. *of the stairs.* CHARLES *joins her and pours out three glasses.*)

How are things in the kitchen ?

NICHOLAS (*moving the armchair to table* R.C.). Looks like a battlefield. Gertrude and Annie are doing a sort of juggling act with the washing-up. Fenny had to cut the sandwiches in mid-air. (*He stoops to flick his trousers with a handkerchief.*)

DORA. What's the matter ?

NICHOLAS. Trod in the cat's saucer of milk.

DORA. Oh dear !

NICHOLAS. It got a good laugh, anyhow.

(MARGERY *comes down with a drink for* NICHOLAS. CHARLES *takes whisky to* DORA *and brings his own.*)

I won't offer you a sandwich, Margery, because it wouldn't be kind.

MARGERY (*down* R. *of the table*). Do you really think I'm heavier ?

NICHOLAS. No—no—not more than a couple of stone.

CHARLES (*sitting on the* R. *arm of the sofa*). You don't take enough exercise. When you were a child you were always curled up in a chair.

NICHOLAS. Couldn't curl up in a chair now, could you, dear ?

DORA.   You really ought to keep an eye on yourself.

NICHOLAS.   What she wants is an eye in the back of her head.

(MARGERY *sits* R. *of the table* R.C.)

Ah well, what's broad in the beam comes out in the bust.   Go on, you know you want one.

(*He hands the sandwiches and she takes one.*)

MARGERY.   Well, just one.

NICHOLAS.   Come on, Fenny.   You must be famished.

FENNY.   I *am* rather hungry.   (*She crosses to the table* R.C. *with a cup of cocoa and sits in the armchair.*)

DORA.   Where's Hilda ?   (*Calling.*)   Hilda——

FENNY (*jumping up*).   I'll just see——

CHARLES (*pushing her down*).   No, no, Fenny.

FENNY.   I'm not a bit tired, really, Mr. Randolph.

NICHOLAS.   Go on, eat your damn bun.

(CYNTHIA *and* EDNA *come downstairs.   * EDNA *goes to the whisky-table and takes a drink.*)

MARGERY.   Hello.

(MARGERY *rises to kiss* CYNTHIA.   *They meet down* R.)

CYNTHIA.   Hello, Marge.   I say, you've put it on a bit.

MARGERY.   You beast, you're slimmer than ever.   Oh well, you haven't had two children.

CYNTHIA.   No, I haven't done that.   How are you, Fenny ?   (*She shakes hands with* FENNY.)   Hello, Nicholas.   (*She kisses* NICHOLAS.)

(MARGERY *moves the chair from the desk to the table.*)

NICHOLAS.   Hello, Fatty.

MARGERY.   My God !

DORA.   Really, Margery.

MARGERY.   Sorry, Mother.   But when I think we used to call Cynthia " Fatty "——

(CYNTHIA *sits below* R. *of the table* R.C. *on the chair from the desk.* MARGERY *stands behind her.*)

EDNA (*helping herself to whisky*).   Oh, Nicholas——

NICHOLAS.   How are you, Edna ?   Sorry I was so taken up with the prodigal daughter.

(CYNTHIA *looks at him quickly.*   MARGERY *sits upstage of* CYNTHIA *and talks to her.*   FENNY *offers sandwiches.*)

EDNA (*coming down* C.).   Can you manage Friday ?   I've got the seats.

NICHOLAS. Friday ? Friday ?—yes, that's quite all right.
Dine with me first, then. Scott's ?

EDNA. I'd like to. (*She crosses and sits in the armchair
down* L.)

NICHOLAS. Better make it seven. (*He takes out a diary,
comes* C., *and writes it down.*)

DORA. It must be very nice for you to have a brother-in-law
to take you out, dear—specially now Hugh's married. (*She
rises to the fender-stool and pours out cocoa.*)

NICHOLAS. I took her out long before Hugh married—or
rather, she took me.

DORA. Cocoa, Cynthia ?

(BELLE *and* BILL *come down the stairs.* BILL *is carrying a large
box of chocolates.*)

CHARLES. Would you rather have whisky ?

DORA. Oh no, she loves cocoa—I had it made specially for her.

CYNTHIA. All right, Mother, I'll have some.

(DORA *gives a cup of cocoa to* CHARLES, *who meets* BILL C. *and
gives it to him.* BILL *goes to* CYNTHIA *with it.* CHARLES *goes
up to the whisky-table.* BELLE *comes down* C.)

DORA. Ah, Belle dear—— This is my daughter-in-law,
Edna——

(FENNY *rises and goes to the whisky-table.*)

BELLE. We met upstairs.

MARGERY (*rising*). I'm Margery.

BELLE. Save us, you were the little skinny one.

MARGERY (*sitting again*). I'm having a loathsome evening.

NICHOLAS (*holding a sandwich*). Aunt Belle, you look marvellous. Let me press a very sardiny kiss on your cheek. (*He
kisses her.*)

(BILL *is showing chocolates to* MARGERY *and* CYNTHIA.)

BELLE. Nicholas—and not married or anything ?

NICHOLAS. I don't know what you mean by " or anything."

DORA. I don't think Nicholas will ever marry. (*She sits on
the sofa.*)

(BELLE *sits in the armchair at the table.*)

EDNA. Neither do I.

NICHOLAS. Let me tell you, I've had my chances.

(FENNY *comes down with a drink for* BELLE.)

EDNA. You're a born bachelor, Nicholas.

BELLE. Is this another daughter-in-law ?

CHARLES. This is our very dear Grace Fenning—Fenny.

DORA. My companion.

NICHOLAS. Don't call her that, Mother—such a dreary name.

FENNY. Won't you have some sandwiches ?

(BELLE *takes a sandwich.* CHARLES *takes* DORA's *glass and goes back to the whisky-table.* FENNY *joins him.*)

MARGERY (*looking at* BILL's *chocolates.*) How kind of Aunt Belle. You must offer them round.

BILL (*eyeing the large party*). Oh, all right. (*Slightly opening the lid.*) Does anyone want one ?

(*There is a murmur of* " No, thank you, Bill.")

Sure ? It's quite all right. Oh, go on, Mummie. You never say no.

(NICHOLAS *laughs, takes a chocolate and puts it in front of* MARGERY.)

MARGERY. Go to bed and stop in bed.

BILL (*crossing to* DORA). Good night, Grannie.

DORA (*kissing him*). Good night, darling. We'll let you off the other good nights.

BILL. Oh, very well. (*He mounts the stairs, then turns.*) Couldn't I wait till Flouncy comes in ?

MARGERY. No. And clean your teeth again after those chocolates.

BILL. I should think my teeth must be jolly near worn away.

(*He disappears upstairs.* HILDA *comes in from the* L.)

DORA. Where on earth have you been ?

HILDA. I told you, Mother, telephoning. (*Crossing* C. *and shaking hands.*) Aunt Belle, how very nice—Cynthia ! (*She goes to* CYNTHIA, *who rises and kisses her.*) What an age it is.

DORA. You weren't really telephoning all that time, Hilda ?

HILDA. Yes, Mother. (*She comes back to* C.)

DORA. But it must have been twenty minutes.

HILDA. Twenty-one. I asked the exchange.

DORA. Really, Hilda ! Do you know what that costs ?

HILDA. Yes, Mother. Six and fivepence. Here it is. (*She offers the money.*)

DORA. I shouldn't dream of taking your money. But really —I never heard anything so extravagant.

HILDA. Then take the money. Either you take the money or you stop calling it extravagant.

DORA. I shan't take the money and I shall call it extravagant. It's just giving the money to the Government.

HILDA. But you like the Government.

DORA. Not all that much.

(CYNTHIA *again offers the money.*)

Put it away, dear.

HILDA. Oh, very well. (*She goes to* L., *above the sofa.*)
DORA. Where are you going now ?
HILDA. I want to make sure I put the receiver on.

(*She goes off* L.)

DORA. And before dinner it was the bathroom taps. (*To*
BELLE.) She went all the way upstairs to see if she turned them
off.

(*There is a laugh from everyone.*)

Really, I don't think she's quite sane.
NICHOLAS. She's sane enough to make a damn good income.

(HILDA *returns and comes to* c.)

DORA. Well, was it on ?
HILDA. Yes.
DORA. Quite sure ?
HILDA. Oh, Mother, don't. (*She suddenly decides to go back
and see.*)
DORA. Hilda, if you go back again I'll have you certified.
For goodness' sake sit down and let us all have some peace.

(HILDA *sits on the back of the sofa.* CHARLES *goes to join her.*)

Edna——

(EDNA *is looking at a magazine.*)

(*Calling cheerfully.*) Edna——

(FENNY *comes to the table to between* CYNTHIA *and* MARGERY.)

EDNA. Yes, Mrs. Randolph ?
DORA. Did you bring the coal-glove back ?
EDNA. No, I'm afraid I didn't.
DORA. Better get it, dear. Then it'll be here when it's
wanted.
EDNA (*sighing*). Very well, Mrs. Randolph. (*She rises, puts
her glass on the mantelpiece and goes to the stairs.*) I had to let
our fire out, Hilda ; it's smoking hopelessly.
HILDA. I don't mind.
EDNA. I'm afraid I do. I'm used to central heating.

(*She disappears.*)

DORA. I'm afraid Edna's just a little put out that she hasn't
got Cynthia's room.
HILDA. Well, she always does have it and I know she hates
sharing.

DORA. Somebody's got to share and it's quite obvious I should give Cynthia her old room.

HILDA. You haven't given me my old room.

(MARGERY *listens*.)

Margery and Kenneth are in it.

MARGERY. You're welcome to my share of it. It isn't a full-size double bed and you know how Kenneth kicks.

(NICHOLAS *listens*.)

DORA. *What* discontented children—grumble, grumble, grumble.

NICHOLAS. " What, grumbling, Mrs. Montmorency ? "

HILDA. Oh, Nicholas.

(*All the family laugh except* CYNTHIA.)

CHARLES. He's dead now, poor man.

BELLE. Who is ?

DORA. The grocer's boy with the squint. It was when Nicholas had measles——

(CYNTHIA *takes a cigarette from the box on the table*.)

NICHOLAS. Never try to explain a family joke, Mother, they sound the merest gibberish. You remember, don't you, Fatty ?

CYNTHIA. Yes, I remember. (*She strikes a match and lights her cigarette*.)

(EDNA *comes downstairs*.)

EDNA. The soot's come down now, Hilda.

DORA. A brick came down that chimney once.

EDNA (*to* HILDA, *as she crosses back to the armchair down* L. *and sits*). It strikes me we shall be very lucky if we're alive in the morning. (*She puts the coal-glove back*.)

(GERTRUDE *enters* L. *with six rubber hot-water bottles and one stone one*.)

FENNY. Do you want me, Gertrude ? (*She crosses to* R. *of* GERTRUDE.)

(*Everyone reacts to* GERTRUDE'S *entrance*.)

GERTRUDE. It's the hot-water bottles, miss. Annie's got them mixed, madam. (*She comes* C.)

DORA. Good gracious, whose is that ? (*She points to one in a satin cover*.)

BELLE. Mine, Dora.

MARGERY. That's mine.

EDNA. That's mine.

HILDA. Gertrude, where's mine ?

GERTRUDE. Annie went and gave it to Miss Scrap.

DORA. Will you have the stone one ?

HILDA. No, Mother. It bruises my toes.

DORA. Well, we can't disturb the child now. It's a splendid stone bottle. And you can warm your toes by the fire.

EDNA. Not by our fire, you can't.

DORA. Very well. I'll have the stone one. Give Miss Hilda my bottle.

(General protest.)

HILDA. Oh no, Mother——

DORA. Not another word. I just want everyone to be happy. You can take them up this way, Gertrude.

GERTRUDE. Thank you, madam.

(GERTRUDE goes up. HILDA runs after her and takes the stone bottle from her. FENNY goes up to the whisky-table.)

DORA. Really, I think it's about time we all made a move.

(BELLE, CYNTHIA and EDNA rise.)

Now, we can manage two hot baths to-night and three to-morrow morning. Will you have yours now, Belle ?

BELLE. Well, if it'll make things easier.

(BELLE turns to the table and talks. FENNY comes to the table and collects plates.)

DORA. And Edna second. You like yours in the morning, Cynthia. And, Nicholas—

(NICHOLAS comes c.)

—will you please not fill the bath to the brim ? We must all remember the washing-up.

NICHOLAS. Don't worry, darling. I had a good soak this morning and I'm not counting on seeing a bath again till I get home on Monday. *(He crosses to the fire and talks to EDNA.)* What beats me is to think of the state of filth we must have lived in as children.

DORA. Nonsense. Don't tell me all these baths people have nowadays are for cleanliness ; they're for fun. Would you run along, Belle dear ?

BELLE. I suppose I'd better say good night.

NICHOLAS. Don't bother, Auntie. We shall go on bumping into each other on landings for hours and hours yet.

BELLE. I'll say a provisional one then.

(They all say " Good night " to her. CHARLES goes to the foot of the stairs with her, then comes down to the table R.C.)

CHARLES *(to FENNY)*. Finished your dress for the dance ?

FENNY. I've still got the hem to turn up.

(CHARLES *picks up two glasses from the table.*)

CYNTHIA. Slip it on and I'll do it for you.

FENNY. Would you really ? But there's still the glass and silver to put away.

(CHARLES *goes up to the whisky-table.*)

DORA. Edna dear, you'll do the glass, won't you ?

EDNA (*resigned*). Very well, Mrs. Randolph. (*She crosses* O.)

FENNY. Are you sure you don't mind ? I would like to wear my dress to-morrow if I could.

(EDNA *goes into the dining-room.*)

NICHOLAS (*to* FENNY). Cut along, we'll do this. (*He crosses to the table* R.C. *with the cocoa-tray.*)

FENNY (*to* CYNTHIA, *as she runs upstairs*). I'll go straight down into the sewing-room.

(FENNY *disappears.*)

DORA (*rising*). I don't believe Edna knows where the best glass goes.

(*She goes into the dining-room.* CYNTHIA *goes up after* DORA *to the whisky-table to fetch the tray.* CHARLES *opens and closes the door for* DORA.)

NICHOLAS (*to* MARGERY). Give us a hand, you, and help to get your weight down.

(NICHOLAS *exits* L. *with the sandwich-tray.* CYNTHIA *exits with the whisky-tray.* MARGERY *exits with the cocoa-tray.* CHARLES *crosses to the fire.* KENNETH *and* FLOUNCY *enter* R.)

CHARLES. Walked your dinner off, Flouncy ?

FLOUNCY. I wish you wouldn't call me Flouncy, Grandpa.

CHARLES. I must try to remember your name's Gwen.

FLOUNCY. I don't like Gwen much better. I think I should like you to call me Guinevere.

KENNETH. I couldn't have a child called Guinevere. You stop being such a vain little peacock and perhaps we'll stop calling you Flouncy.

FLOUNCY. I'm not vain. If Grannie sends me any goloshes I shan't wear them. (*She throws her goloshes across the room.*)

(CHARLES *crosses to pick up the goloshes.*)

KENNETH. You hop off to bed. Come on, I'll take your coat. (*He takes off her coat up* O.) I think I walked her a bit far.

(MARGERY *enters* L.)

CHARLES. I'm sure Kenneth wants some whisky.

MARGERY. It's in the pantry. Get it yourself, Ken, and then slip up the back way.

(MARGERY *takes the coat from* KENNETH *and pushes him off* L. CHARLES *gives him the goloshes over the back of the sofa.*)

Mother's in a job-finding mood.

(KENNETH *nods and goes off* L.)

I'm sorry, Father, but she is.

FLOUNCY (*sitting on the stairs, wailing*). Oh, Mummie, I've gone tired.

MARGERY. Well, go to bed.

FLOUNCY. I'm too tired to go to bed.

MARGERY. Get along, or your Grannie'll catch us. (*Whispering.*) Good night, Father. (*To* FLOUNCY.) I won't bother to curl your hair to-night.

FLOUNCY. But I must have curly hair for the party. (*Wailing.*) Oh, Mummie, I do wish you'd let me have a permanent wave.

(*They disappear upstairs.* CHARLES *goes off* L. *as* DORA *returns from the dining-room.*)

DORA (*to* EDNA, *within.*) Yes, dear, on the very top shelf. Good gracious, where is everyone ? People just slide away. (*Calling.*) Margery—I want her to——

CHARLES. Not to-night, dear. You'll be worn out. Just come along to bed.

DORA. Perhaps I will. I do want to be fresh for to-morrow. (*She collects various belongings.*) Did you notice how stiff she was ?

CHARLES. Who ?

DORA. Belle, of course. Those stairs gave her a bit of trouble. You can have your face lifted, but you've still got to lift your own legs.

(CHARLES *crosses* R. *and turns out the lamp on the desk.*)

Are you going to lock up ?

CHARLES. I'll come down. Hugh and Laurel are still out. (*He goes up and turns out the lamp on the bookshelves, then takes his book from a shelf.*)

DORA (*ascending the stairs briskly*). I'm thankful to say stairs have never been any trouble to me. I believe she's seventy-seven.

(DORA *and* CHARLES *exit up the stairs.* HUGH *and* LAUREL *come in through the front door.*)

LAUREL. Hello—have they all gone to bed ?

HUGH. Quite probably. Rather a good job. (*Taking off his*

B

coat.) You must find them a bit overpowering. (*He puts his coat on the armchair* c.)

LAUREL. Me ? Your family ? I adore them. I adore everything here—the house, the village and those heavenly illegitimate Tupkinses. (*She shivers.*) I'm quite cold. (*She crosses to the fender-stool, takes the bellows and blows the fire.*) I'm crazy about large families.

HUGH (*taking the bellows from her and blowing up the fire*). That's because you're an only child.

(LAUREL *pulls out the fender-stool, sits and lets her coat fall off.*)

LAUREL. I daresay. I wish I had ancestors.

HUGH. Well, of course you have.

LAUREL. No. People who are born in flats don't have ancestors. Were you born here ?

HUGH. Yes.

LAUREL. And your father and your grandfather and your great-grandfather—and *his* father ?

HUGH. Not him ; he built it.

LAUREL. Who'll it come to eventually ?

HUGH. No one, I should think. It'll just be sold.

LAUREL. But that's not right. Your father was the eldest son. Why isn't it entailed ?

HUGH. Good lord, it isn't one of the stately homes of England. I can't think of a worse fate than having to live in it.

LAUREL. But don't you see how romantic it is ? Think, baby's great-great-great-grandfather——

HUGH. He was a draper in Colchester. Do you get much of a kick out of that ?

LAUREL. Was your grandfather a draper too ?

HUGH. I believe he kept an eye on the business when first he and Grannie were married. But he retired before he was forty.

LAUREL. Do you mean he hasn't done anything at all for all these years ?

HUGH. I expect Grannie found him a few nice little jobs.

(LAUREL *looks up at the portrait over the mantelpiece.*)

What are you looking at ?

LAUREL. Your father's picture. He was exactly your age when he was killed in the War.

HUGH. Come on, face—— Ready for bed ?

LAUREL (*picking up her coat and going to the stairs*). I suppose so. Are there any more family to see ?

HUGH. Old Belle—I expect she's arrived. And Cynthia.

LAUREL. Oh, the dark horse.

HUGH. Shut up. Grannie doesn't know about that. I suppose I'd better turn this out. (*He turns out the remaining lamp, puts the stool back, takes his coat from the armchair c. and joins* LAUREL *on the stairs.*)

LAUREL. We must have a look at baby. Oh, Hugh, isn't it thrilling to think he's sleeping in your father's nursery, with your father's old nurse looking after him ?

(*They go upstairs.*)

HUGH. It's a jolly sight more thrilling to think it won't be us he'll wake up in the middle of the night.

(*After a second* CYNTHIA *comes from* L. *and walks slowly upstairs. At the bend she turns and looks down into the fire-lit room, then continues up.* FENNY *comes in from* L. NICHOLAS *comes through the front door at almost the same moment.* FENNY *is in a dressing-gown and carries a white dress on her arm.*)

FENNY. Hello, where have you been ? (*She joins him down* c.)

NICHOLAS. Putting the car away. Is that the dress ?

FENNY. Mind the pins in the hem. Cynthia's going to sew it for me to-morrow.

NICHOLAS. Funny, I don't ever remember you in evening dress.

FENNY. You've seen me every Christmas. They've mostly been black.

NICHOLAS. Of course. I do remember vaguely. Do you know what I remember you in best ? A grey flannel suit and a hat like a little pork pie. You wore it the first day you came here.

FENNY. Fancy you remembering.

NICHOLAS. You stood there in the doorway, clutching a sort of gladstone bag—looking exactly like little Orphan Annie.

FENNY. I felt a bit like her. You were all at tea. I thought you were the most superb family I had ever seen.

NICHOLAS. And what do you think of us after—how long ? Seven, eight——

FENNY. Ten years. Oh, you're not so bad. (*She takes one step up* c.)

NICHOLAS. But seriously. Sit down a minute, I feel like talking.

(FENNY *crosses to the fender-stool and sits.* NICHOLAS *goes to the* L. *arm of the sofa and sits. They both face the fire, which is bright enough to illuminate their faces.*)

I was walking round the garden just now, looking at all the bedroom windows lighted up. There's something rather heart-breaking about family gatherings.

FENNY. How do you mean ?

NICHOLAS. Oh, I dunno exactly. I suppose they make you realize the shortness of life—old age simply rushing at one. You know, once one stops being a child, time seems to get the bit between its teeth. Do you know, I'm nearly thirty-five ?

FENNY. That isn't very old.

NICHOLAS. But I've *done* nothing yet.

FENNY. Don't you like your job ?

NICHOLAS. Oh yes—advertising's interesting enough, especially now I'm a director. And I've a good many other irons in the fire. It's nothing to do with concrete success. I suppose it's some sort of spiritual lack. (*Moving to c. of the sofa.*) Oh, hark at me !

FENNY. Don't make fun of yourself. I wish I could understand.

NICHOLAS. Oh, I always get these broody fits when I come home. We used to be such a nice-looking lot of kids, and look at us now—Margery fat as a barrel, Hilda getting completely desiccated, and Cynthia sitting about registering the woman with a past.

FENNY. Oh, Nicholas, don't. I don't see any of them like that. And look at your father and mother—haven't they grown old beautifully ?

NICHOLAS. Nothing grows old beautifully. Aunt Belle's a scream, isn't she ? Just held together with sticking-plaster.

FENNY. You are the most extraordinary person. I've never known anyone else who was so kind-hearted and yet so malicious.

NICHOLAS. Am I often malicious ?

FENNY. Quite a bit. I wonder if you could be cruel ?

NICHOLAS. I expect so. How clever of you to find me out. I always take a vow on the threshold to be the sunny boy of the party.

FENNY. You usually are, too.

NICHOLAS. Oh, the family, the family—I can never quite make up my mind whether I love it or loathe it. I believe I'd rather give fifty pounds than come to these gatherings of the clan.

FENNY. Rubbish ! You like them really.

NICHOLAS. I wonder if you're right. They've got some sort of horrible fascination, even if they do start me thinking of death and worms. Do you know, when I was a kid, it used to infuriate me to think that this house—that any inanimate thing —could go on long after me. I say, why *do* you let me drivel on like this ? Edna would have given me a kick in the pants long ago.

FENNY. Would she ?

NICHOLAS. Oh, Edna's very good for me. I wonder if old Peter'll look down on our grand family dinner on Sunday. My God, I've got a nerve to sentimentalize about the tragedy of

growing old. Do you know, I only missed the War by inches.
Here, what time do you get up in the morning ?

FENNY. About seven.

NICHOLAS. I am a thoughtless swine. You pop off to bed.
You're a very sweet person, Fenny. You look about fourteen
sitting there in your dressing-gown.

FENNY. I'm twenty-nine.

NICHOLAS. Crikey, are you ? Don't you ever regret the
years you've spent with this dreary family ?

FENNY. Not one of them. And it's not dreary.—I'm sorry
I said you were malicious.

NICHOLAS. My dear, it's perfectly true. But I don't think
I could ever be malicious about you. (*He takes her hand and
rubs it.*) That poor hand—just like a little nutmeg-grater.
Dear Fenny.

(EDNA *comes from the dining-room.*)

Hello, Edna—come and get warm.

EDNA. No, thanks. (*She comes down* O., *then pauses.*)

NICHOLAS (*to* FENNY). Here, you hop off to bed. You'll be
dog-tired in the morning. Up-sy-daisy. (*He pulls her up.*)
Legs tired ?

FENNY. A bit. (*She picks up her dress.*)

NICHOLAS. Shall I carry you ?

FENNY (*laughing*). Of course not. (*She goes to the stairs.*)
Good night, Edna.

EDNA. Good night.

NICHOLAS. Good night, my dear.

FENNY (*on the stairs*). Good night, Nicholas.

EDNA (*as soon as* FENNY *is out of sight*). Nicholas, I call that
the limit. Sitting holding Fenny's hand in the firelight.

NICHOLAS. Have you gone out of your senses ?

EDNA. I know it's just sheer thoughtlessness—unless—I
suppose you don't happen to be in love with her ?

NICHOLAS. Good God, no.

EDNA. Then you might have a little imagination.

CHARLES (*off* L.). Nicholas, will you lock up ?

NICHOLAS. Very well, Father.

CHARLES. And see to the fire.

NICHOLAS. I will.

(EDNA *goes towards the stairs.*)

One minute, Edna. What did you mean just now ?

EDNA. If you really don't know—— Perhaps I was just
being officious. Good night.

(*She goes up the stairs and off.*)

NICHOLAS. Good night, Edna.

(NICHOLAS *stands for a moment, thinking. Then he moves the ferder-stool and turns back the hearth-rug. He crosses to the front door and pushes home the top bolt.*)

BILL (*off* L., *singing shrilly*). Good King Wenceslas looked out, on the feast of Stephen.
CHARLES (*off* L.). Quiet, Bill.
BILL (*off* L.). Sorry, Grandpa, I thought it was Christmas.

NICHOLAS *bolts the lower bolt. The clock starts to strike eleven. He crosses to the stairs. The glow from the fire is now very faint, but the staircase is clearly lit by the lamp held by the plaster figure :* NICHOLAS *turns it out, and as he goes upstairs—*

The CURTAIN *falls.*

ACT II

SCENE 1

SCENE.—*The Nursery. A pleasant, sunny room, with plush window-curtains, yellowed white paint and a faded Caldicott wallpaper depicting John Gilpin's adventures; a room that remembers three earlier generations of children.*

There is a fireplace R. with a high fireguard. Below this is a small service lift. There is a very large, high toy-cupboard in the R. corner of the room with a small step-ladder near it. R.C. of the back wall is a big bow-window with a window-seat; a rocking-horse stands between it and the door to the landing, which is in the L. of the back wall. Some low shelves, piled with books, toys and oddments are on the L. of this door. Then, in the L. wall is the door to the night-nurseries, and below this an upright piano. The furniture includes a large table C., with chairs round it.

(See Photograph of Scene.)

It is Saturday morning. NANNY PATCHING, *a comfortable-looking woman of sixty-two, is finishing breakfast with* FLOUNCY, SCRAP *and* BILL. NANNY *is above the table, with* SCRAP *on her* R. *and* FLOUNCY *on her* L. BILL *is below* FLOUNCY.

SCRAP (*holding her mug*). I like mugs. Did they always have mugs in this nursery ?

NANNY. Always, Miss Scrap.

BILL. This is the very same mug that Mummie had, isn't it, Nanny ?

SCRAP. Which mug did my Mummie have ?

NANNY. Let me see now—some of them got broken, of course. Your mother had a bluebird mug.

SCRAP. Do you mean it might have been this very one ?

NANNY. Sure to have been.

(SCRAP *looks at her mug lovingly.*)

Now don't you go thinking about it. Your mother wouldn't want you to brood.

SCRAP. But I like thinking about it.

NANNY. That's enough, dear. Finish your milk.

BILL. Oh, hurry up, hurry up. I want to paint. (*He rises.*)

NANNY (*restraining him*). No, you don't, Master Bill.

(BILL *returns to his seat.*)

We say grace in this nursery. " For what we have received may the Lord make us truly thankful. Amen."

SCRAP. Amen.

FLOUNCY (*intoning slightly*). Amen.

BILL (*intoning heavily*). Selfridge's.

SCRAP. Why did you say that ?

BILL (*casually*). I always do.

NANNY. He's a very naughty boy.

BILL. Come on, let's clear the table. (*He takes bread and marmalade to the lift.*)

NANNY. Careful of that lift, now.

(FLOUNCY *takes the teapot and hot-water jug to the lift.* NANNY *starts to clear on to the tray.* SCRAP *helps* NANNY. *After* BILL *has puts his things in the lift, he takes the hot-water jug from* FLOUNCY, *goes to the cupboard, takes out a cup and fills it.*

HUGH *and* LAUREL *enter from the landing.*)

HUGH. Hello, Nanny. Has he been good ?

NANNY. I never knew such a good baby. Good morning, madam.

LAUREL. Shall we take him for a bit now ?

NANNY. I'd be glad if you would. I want to run down to the kitchen.

(SCRAP *takes the tray to* FLOUNCY *at the lift.* FLOUNCY *puts it on the lift, then goes to the window-seat, gets a magazine from the cupboard under it and takes them to the table.* SCRAP *goes back* C. *and helps* NANNY *fold the tablecloth.* NANNY *puts the cloth and napkins in the drawer of the table.*)

LAUREL (*looking through the night-nursery door*). He's just waking up.

(*She goes in.*)

NANNY. He had a lovely sleep after his bottle.

(HUGH *goes in after* LAUREL. *The lift is stacked.*)

BILL (*pushing* FLOUNCY *away from the lift and putting in the hot-water jug*). Oh ! come on, Guinevere.

NANNY (*folding the tablecloth*). Miss Scrap, will you help me ?

BILL (*blowing down the speaking-tube*). Good morning, Cook— how's your varicose veins ? . . . Really ? I'll be down. (*He replaces the whistle in the tube.*) She's got her elastic stocking on.

(*The lift goes down.*)

(*He crosses with his paint-box and the cup of water.*) We'd better have the glass too.

NANNY. Miss Scrap's rose is in it.

FLOUNCY. I'll throw it out, it's dead. (*She picks the glass up.*)

SCRAP. No, it isn't—not quite. Please don't.

NANNY. Leave it alone—you can manage with the cup. (*She puts* FLOUNCY *in the chair at the top of the table and moves the chair from up* L. *of the table to up stage of the piano.*)

BILL. What'll you have, Flouncy ? " Fashions " ? And I'll have " Country Life." Choose one for yourself, Scrap.

(*The children are now seated at the table :* FLOUNCY *above*, SCRAP R., BILL L.)

NANNY. You won't get long for your painting—we'll be going out walking in no time. (*She goes to the night-nursery door.*) Mr. Hugh—— They've gone down. (*Turning.*) I'll be back for you children in a quarter of an hour.

(*She goes off into the night-nursery.*)

BILL (*licking his brush and settling to his painting*). *I* may be going out with Great-aunt Belle. She wants to know what I said at school.

SCRAP (*choosing a magazine*). What *did* you say at school ?

FLOUNCY. He said Damn Blast Devil Hell and Strike me Pink.

BILL (*pushing* FLOUNCY). You beast, Flouncy. It's **my** language. I tell it. I said Swelp me, too.

SCRAP. Swelp you ? What does it mean ?

BILL. Something frightful.

SCRAP. I don't think much of it. I know a worse word than any of those.

FLOUNCY. You don't.

BILL. What is it ?

SCRAP. I couldn't tell you. It's too awful.

BILL. Oh, go on, Scrap.

FLOUNCY. She's just pretending.

SCRAP. I'm not pretending. It's the most terrible word there is. (*She looks round nervously, then whispers hoarsely.*) It's District Nurse.

BILL. District Nurse ? But they put that on gates.

FLOUNCY. You silly baby. Everyone knows what District Nurse means.

BILL. It might have a double meaning, Flouncy.

FLOUNCY. Of course it hasn't.

BILL. I'm afraid you've got it wrong, Scrap—but I'll find out. I say, Flouncy, you've made this water filthy. You can use any colours you like, Scrap, except the cobalt blue. That's my special colour.

SCRAP (*frigidly*). **I** don't want your beastly cobalt and it *is* an awful word.

BILL. All right, all right. I told you I'd find out. I'm putting my brush in my mouth over and over again. I'll probably die.

(*Voices are heard outside.* MARGERY, KENNETH *and* NICHOLAS *enter from the landing.* MARGERY *goes to* BILL, KENNETH *up behind* FLOUNCY, *and* NICHOLAS *to behind* SCRAP.)

MARGERY. Isn't Nanny taking you for a walk?
BILL. Presently. We're just using my new paint-box.
KENNETH. I say, that is a beauty.
FLOUNCY. Do you know Scrap, Uncle Nicholas?
NICHOLAS. Yes. I looked in on her last night. (*He looks over* SCRAP'S *shoulder.*)
MARGERY. Careful, Bill—you're running your trees into your sky.

(*She takes his brush. There is a mute protest from* BILL.)

There! Just saved it. Look, you want to carry that blob of paint right down——

(MARGERY *pushes* BILL *off his chair and sits.* BILL *wanders to the piano-stool.*)

KENNETH (*behind* FLOUNCY). You can't have them all in black. Give them some red buttons—and red heels to their shoes. Here, budge up a bit. (*He sits beside her and paints, gradually edging* FLOUNCY *off.*)
NICHOLAS (*over* SCRAP'S *book*). Why don't you make that one a zebra?
SCRAP. Because it's a horse.
NICHOLAS. But you could make it a zebra with some white stripes. Look, we'll use some chinese white. We'll use oodles of chinese white. We'll give him lovely stripes. Come on, Scrap. (*He starts to paint.*)
KENNETH (*who has completely edged* FLOUNCY *off her chair*). I've given her a jolly old red hat. Why don't you have a red hat, Margery?

(FLOUNCY *goes to the rocking-horse.*)

MARGERY. Half a minute, Ken—this is quite difficult.
NICHOLAS. That's marvellous. I used to be awfully good at this. Just a second, Scrap, while I get under his stomach.

(*He takes* SCRAP'S *place.* SCRAP *goes to the arm of the armchair.*)

KENNETH. I often think I ought to have gone in for art.
MARGERY. There—I don't think that's too bad. (*She turns the page.*) Oh, there's a beauty on the next page.
BILL. Mummie, wouldn't you like to play the piano? (*Get-*

ting no reply, he goes over to her.)　Oh, darling, you've smudged it.　You are a clumsy old cow.

MARGERY (*swinging round on* BILL, *who springs back*).　Bill! Never let me hear you use that word again.

BILL.　What word?　Clumsy?

MARGERY.　No.　Cow.　You must *not* call me a cow.

BILL.　But you don't mind me calling you a donkey.

MARGERY.　I'm not really keen on it.　And anyhow, cow's different.　You must never call anyone a cow.

BILL.　Can't I call a cow a cow?

MARGERY (*to* KENNETH).　It's really very difficult.—You can call a cow a cow, but you must never call a lady a cow.　Now go and get ready for your walk.

KENNETH.　You'll understand when you're older, old chap. It's a sort of double meaning.

BILL.　Golly—a nice little word like cow.　Perhaps you're right, Scrap.　(*He looks meaningly at* SCRAP, *who signals to try to stop him, then plants his feet wide apart and looks at the ceiling.*) District Nurse.　(*Louder.*)　District Nurse.

MARGERY.　Well, what about the district nurse?

BILL.　Don't you mind me saying it?

MARGERY.　Not if it gives you any pleasure.　It's very silly, of course.

BILL (*with a gesture*).　Told you so, Scrap.

(*He goes off* L. *into the night-nursery.*)

MARGERY.　Run along or you'll keep Nanny waiting.

(SCRAP *and* FLOUNCY *follow* BILL.　SCRAP *shuts the door after her.*)

Kenneth, how heavily you're breathing.

KENNETH (*sitting back*).　I've given the whole bally lot of them red hats.

(DORA'S *voice calls* "Margery.")

MARGERY.　Is that Mother calling?

(FENNY *enters from the landing and comes to the top of the table.*)

Did I hear Mother?

FENNY.　I'm afraid so.　She wants extra eggs from Malting's Farm.

MARGERY.　No, I'm damned if I'll go.　(*Rising to the door up* L.)　There's no car road and it's in a sea of mud.　Come on, Ken, we'll slip down the back-stairs and hide in the greenhouse.

(KENNETH *rises and follows her.*)

Don't give us away, Fenny.

(*She hustles* KENNETH *off* L.　FENNY *goes to the shelves* L.)

NICHOLAS (*rising*). Good old Margery. She always was the champion job-evader. (*He goes over to the window-seat and sits.*) I feel very well disposed towards the world.

FENNY (*rummaging on the shelves by the door*). Do you ?

NICHOLAS. Wakened up feeling absolutely sunny.

FENNY. Good. You were a bit on the morbid side last night.

NICHOLAS. Oh, that's all gone. I lay awake this morning, smelling coffee and bacon being cooked, and felt that things were exactly as they should be. Youth, age, birth, death, the changing seasons—I assure you I had the key to the whole damn works.

FENNY. How very useful. (*She crosses to the toy cupboard, pushing the armchair well down by the fire.*)

NICHOLAS. Now don't flatten me. One so seldom has these moments of illumination. (*He goes to the rocking-horse and mounts it.*) This one seems to be quite lasting, too. Yes, I feel positively glowing with human kindness.

(FENNY *turns and laughs at him.*)

I wonder why ? What are you looking for ?

FENNY. Some french chalk to make the drawing-room floor slippery.

NICHOLAS. I say, don't overdo it. It's horse's work keeping those Vicarage girls on their feet.

(*Another laugh from* FENNY.)

Why *will* Mother give dances ?

FENNY. There'll be three tables of whist.

NICHOLAS. Whist ? Can you play whist ?

FENNY. Certainly. I shall probably have to.

NICHOLAS. Oh no, you're going to dance with me. Does Mother still insist on dance programmes ?

FENNY. She does. They've got wedding bells on them.

NICHOLAS. Then I shall bag six dances and we'll sit out on the back-stairs.

FENNY. Last time I sat out on the back-stairs I got kissed on the ear.

NICHOLAS. Fenny ! Who by ?

FENNY. The curate with the wig.

NICHOLAS. I knew you had a past.

FENNY. I know this stuff's somewhere. (*She jumps, trying to see the top shelf.*) This is a ridiculous cupboard for a nursery. (*She drags up the step-ladder and mounts it.*)

NICHOLAS. It had its uses. The best toys were kept on the top shelf. Here, be careful. (*He gets off the horse.*)

FENNY. Pooh ! You should have seen me washing all this paint yesterday. I'm very nifty on a step-ladder.

NICHOLAS. I got marooned up there for an afternoon, when I was about four.

FENNY. How do you mean ?

NICHOLAS. Sit on the top.

(FENNY *sits on the top of the cupboard.*)

The steps were about for spring-cleaning, so up I went—and Cynthia came and moved them—so. (*He moves the steps away.*)

FENNY. You poor kid. It's quite a long way.

NICHOLAS. " Come down, oh maid, from yonder mountain height."

FENNY. Well, give me the steps.

(*They laugh together.*)

Here, come on, I can't stop dallying here.

NICHOLAS (*strolling away*). I think I shall go for a walk.

FENNY. Oh, come on. All right, I'm going to jump.

NICHOLAS. No—no, Fenny, it's much too far. (*He goes to her and puts his hands up to her waist.*) Now you can. (*He jumps her down.*) Has the curate with the wig left you with any inhibitions about being kissed on the ear ?

FENNY. I don't know.

NICHOLAS. Then you should find out. (*He hears sounds in the night-nursery.*) On the back-stairs—remember, it's an assignation.

(*He goes back to the table and paints.* FENNY *puts the armchair straight.* NANNY *and the three children come in from the night-nursery, dressed for walking. First* BILL, *who goes to the table and washes out his mother's painting. Then* SCRAP, *who goes to the landing door. Thirdly* NANNY, *followed by* FLOUNCY.)

NANNY. Anything you want from the village, miss ?

FENNY. Yes, Nanny—try to get some french chalk.

BILL. Let's go in the woods, Nanny.

NANNY. And me with the perambulator ? Get along with you.

(*She bustles off with the girls.* FLOUNCY *and* SCRAP *precede her,* FLOUNCY *arranging her curls with the aid of a mirror from her miniature handbag.*)

BILL (*pulling* NICHOLAS's *arm*). Take us in the woods, Uncle Nick ?

NICHOLAS. Will you come, Fenny ?

FENNY. I'm up to my eyes in jobs.

(NICHOLAS *smiles at her, then allows* BILL *to pull him off.*)

BILL (*as they go*). Come on, come on—we'll give the others the slip.

NICHOLAS. All right. All right.

(*Alone*, FENNY *puts her hands to her cheeks, looking slightly dazed. She goes to the mirror and looks at herself.* BILL *comes back.*)

BILL. I want the blackberry basket. (*He gets the basket from the shelves* L., *then comes* C.) Fenny, you do look nice to-day.

FENNY. Do I, Bill, do I ? I wish I was coming black-berrying.

BILL. Never mind. I'll have a dance with you to-night.

FENNY. You can have it now, if you like. (*She catches his hands and whirls him round.*)

BILL (*breathless, but pleased*). Oh, Fenny, you are fun. I'll bring you some blackberries back.

(*He goes out.* FENNY, *looking radiantly happy, goes to look at what* NICHOLAS *was painting.* EDNA *enters.*)

EDNA. Have you seen Nicholas ?

FENNY. He's gone with the children. Oh, do come and look at the zebra he's been painting.

EDNA. Are you all right, Fenny—you look so flushed.

FENNY. Never felt better in my life.

EDNA. Has Nicholas just left here ?

FENNY. A second ago. You'll catch him if you're quick.

EDNA. I don't think I'll bother.

FENNY (*laughing*). He's put bows on their tails.

EDNA. Oh, my dear——

FENNY (*surprised at her tone*). What ?

EDNA. Fenny, please don't think I mean to be officious, but I know how you feel about Nicholas, we all know——

FENNY. What do you know ?

EDNA. Oh, my dear, don't look like that, there's nothing whatever to be ashamed of. But he's so thoughtless and—well, I'm just not going to stand by and let you make a fool of yourself.

FENNY. How dare you !

EDNA. Fenny——

FENNY. How dare you ! How dare you !

EDNA. Please don't speak to me like that. I'm terribly sorry I spoke. I've done it clumsily.

FENNY (*utterly stricken—turning away to the armchair*). Yes, you have. Oh, how *can* everyone know—I've never told any-one. (*After a pause.*) Does *he* know ?

EDNA. No. I always thought he did, but something he said last night—that's why I spoke to you. (*She comes above the table to above* R. *corner of it.*) You see, my dear, if he knew you cared for him he'd be on his guard, he'd be careful not to—oh, you know what I mean. But as it is—I know him so well, Fenny, he's got such easy, affectionate manners—any unsophisticated woman might think—— You did, didn't you, Fenny ?

(FENNY *turns away.* EDNA *turns to the table and puts a chair in.*)

I knew I was right.

FENNY. Please go away, Edna.

EDNA (*coming back to the attack*). I wish I'd spoken earlier. All these wasted years, slaving in this house ! You're intelligent, Fenny, you could have come up to London, got a good job——

FENNY (*facing her*). What sort of a job ? I haven't any training—and I never wanted to come to London. I've been happy here. There's always been something to look forward to. Edna——

EDNA. Yes ?

FENNY. You do know him terribly well, don't you ? You'd be sure to know if—if——

EDNA. If he cared for you ? (*She goes to* FENNY *and lays a hand on her.*) Fenny, he's confided in me for years—even over silly little temporary attachments. He wouldn't keep a thing like that from me.

FENNY. No. I believe that.

EDNA (*turning up to the table*). How dense men are. I saw in a flash last night that you were getting the wrong impression. I'm desperately sorry for you. Will you let me pay for some training for you ?

FENNY. No.

EDNA. You'll stop on here ?

FENNY. I don't know what I shall do. I ought to get on with my work. (*Trying to pass her.*) Mrs. Randolph will be wanting me.

EDNA. Stay here a bit. I'll go and dance attendance on her. (*Going up to the door.*) My dear, I'm so sorry.

FENNY. That's all right. I've been a fool. It was kindest to tell me.

EDNA. You keep quiet till you feel a little better.

(*She goes out.* FENNY *looks at the cupboard, remembering, then goes up to the window.* CYNTHIA *enters from the night-nursery, carrying a plate of cakes.*)

CYNTHIA. Where's the little Scrap child ? (*She puts the cakes on the table.*)

FENNY. They're all out walking.

CYNTHIA. I got some hot cakes from cook. Like one ?

FENNY. No, thank you.

CYNTHIA. What's the matter ?

FENNY. Nothing. (*She moves down to the armchair.*)

CYNTHIA. What is it ? Has Mother been overworking you ?

FENNY. No—it's nothing. (*She suddenly drops into the armchair and bursts into tears.*)

CYNTHIA (*running to her and putting her arm round her*). Fenny darling—whatever is it ?

FENNY. She said everyone knew.

CYNTHIA. Knew what ? (*She kneels by* FENNY.)

(HILDA *enters from the landing carrying a book. She comes down* L.)

HILDA. Fenny, Mother wants you to——

CYNTHIA. Then she'll have to want. Fenny's upset.

HILDA (*coming over*). Fenny dear ! What *is* the matter ? Is it Nicholas ? He doesn't mean to be unkind.

FENNY. He hasn't been unkind. Oh, you did know !

HILDA. That you're fond of him ? There's no harm in that, is there ?

FENNY. You didn't know, did you, Cynthia ? You couldn't, you haven't been home for years——

CYNTHIA. I used to think you were a bit smitten with him. Has it been going on all these years ? Lord, how unhappy you must have been.

FENNY. I've never been unhappy. I've loved my life here. Edna seems to think I ought to have been a typist or something. I don't want to be a typist. People have been good to me here. And he's always been kind.

CYNTHIA. But only kind ?

FENNY. I suppose so. But just lately—last night, this morning—he was different somehow. I thought—— But I'm what Edna calls an unsophisticated woman. I've just made a fool of myself.

HILDA. Do you mean Edna actually had the cheek to——

FENNY. I think she meant it kindly.

(HILDA *turns away to the table.*)

I suppose the servants know and the children——

HILDA. Nonsense, Fenny. (*She sits at the table and puts her book down.*)

FENNY. Perhaps Nicholas knows all the time and is just pitying me—she says he doesn't, but I expect she'll tell him.

HILDA. Oh, no, she won't—we'll take care of that. Now buck up, old dear.

FENNY (*rising to* C.—*making a real effort*). I know. Sorry I'm making such an ass of myself. Oh, lord, I haven't cried for years.

(CYNTHIA *rises.*)

And there are dozens of jobs waiting for me. Oh, if only she'd waited till after this week-end ! How *am* I going to get through ?

(MARGERY *enters from the landing with some dance programmes.* FENNY *dives into the night-nursery.*)

MARGERY. What's up with Fenny ?

(HILDA *rises.*)

CYNTHIA. Come in a minute and shut the door.

MARGERY. Mother wants the bells on the dance programmes painted gold. It's a nice peaceful job and I'm going to take a long time over it. (*She settles at the table to paint.*)

CYNTHIA (*coming to the top of the table*). Did *you* know Fenny was in love with Nicholas ?

MARGERY. Yes, of course. Has she gone violent or something ?

HILDA. It's Edna. As far as I can make out, she's been warning Fenny off. (*She picks up the book and sits in the arm-chair by the fire.*)

MARGERY. What damned cheek.

CYNTHIA (*sitting at the table*). Is there anything between Nicholas and Edna ?

MARGERY. Good lord, no. She's years older than he is. Besides, Edna's an iceberg. I always think she had Hugh by a correspondence course.

HILDA. She's managed to scare other women out of Nicholas's life pretty effectively. It's jolly convenient to have a good-looking young man to trot you round London. (*She blows into her book before turning the page.*)

CYNTHIA. What are you doing ?

HILDA. I always imagine tiny flies will get shut in books.

CYNTHIA. Are you so fond of flies ?

HILDA. Not in the least. It's one of my things like turning bath-taps off.

MARGERY. Mother's right about you. You're bats.

HILDA. I know. I get worse every day. (*She blows again.*)

MARGERY. I'm using all Bill's gold paint.

CYNTHIA. Haven't either of you any feelings for Fenny at all ?

MARGERY. Of course we have—but it's not quite the novelty to us that it is to you. I've been sorry for her for years. Though, really, I think she's been pretty happy.

CYNTHIA. That's what she said.

MARGERY. Just seeing him occasionally. Of course, he's always been very fond of her.

CYNTHIA. Really fond ?

MARGERY. Oh, not what *you'd* call fond. She's just a piece of family furniture to him.

CYNTHIA. We must get her away from here. You could give her a job in your office, Hilda.

HILDA. What do you suppose we do in my office—make beds and mend stockings ?

(CYNTHIA *rises, stamps and goes up stage.*)

It's no good getting intense about it, Cynthia. She'd be miserable if she left here.

MARGERY. It'll all blow over, Fatty.

CYNTHIA (*coming back to the table*). I tell you she was absolutely heartbroken.

MARGERY. Why now, more than always ?

CYNTHIA. Because the whole thing's come out into the open. And she's terrified that Nicholas knows. Any girl with any pride——

HILDA. I do see that.

MARGERY. Of course, I never had any pride. I just *twined* myself round Kenneth. Well, if Nicholas does suspect, she must show him he's wrong. Tell her to flirt with the lads of the village to-night. Tell you what, I'll lend her Kenneth—he rather admires her.

HILDA. Do you mean you'd put him wise ?

MARGERY. There isn't any need. Ken'll carry on with anyone who crooks their little finger at him.

HILDA. Don't you mind ?

MARGERY. Not in the least. I know what happens to the husbands that don't carry on. You see nature in the raw at our Golf Club.

CYNTHIA. I wonder if she could carry it off ?

MARGERY. Of course she can—she's got quite a bit of spirit. It won't really take Nicholas in if he has spotted her, but she'll think it will and then she can settle down to another ten years patient adoration.

CYNTHIA (*banging a book on the table*). Oh, damn that blasted Edna !

(HILDA *blows into her book.*)

Hilda, if you blow into that book again I shall strike you.

HILDA. It really takes all the pleasure out of reading.

(BILL *enters from the landing.*)

MARGERY. Why aren't you with Nanny ?

BILL. Because I was with Uncle Nick—only Grannie's collared him to drive into Colchester. So I've just been round the paddock by myself. (*He comes round the table to* C.) Where's Fenny ? I've brought her some blackberries.

CYNTHIA. I wouldn't worry her now, Bill. Fenny's not feeling awfully well.

BILL. How very extraordinary. Last time I saw her she was dancing.

CURTAIN.

SCENE 2

SCENE.—*The Nursery. It is mid-afternoon.*

When the CURTAIN *rises,* CYNTHIA *is sitting by the fire, sewing the hem of* FENNY'S *dress.* SCRAP *enters from the landing. She sees* CYNTHIA *is there and starts to go out again.*

CYNTHIA. Hello, Scrap. Come and sit by the fire.

SCRAP. I'm not cold, thank you. (*She comes down* R. *of the table.*) Are you going to wear that dress to-night ?

CYNTHIA. No, it's Fenny's. Why ?

SCRAP. I just thought it looked a nice sort of dress. It's a bit like one Mummie used to wear.

CYNTHIA (*looking at* SCRAP). She always liked soft, pretty dresses.

SCRAP. Yes. (*Crossing to* CYNTHIA.) Auntie Cynthia——

CYNTHIA. Yes, Scrap ?

SCRAP. There was a photograph of her and you in dresses made exactly alike, with lots of frills on.

CYNTHIA. I remember. It was taken on our twenty-first birthday. We looked quite a bit alike in that photograph.

SCRAP. Yes, I thought you did. But I suppose it was only the dresses. You're not a bit like her really. That's funny, isn't it ? I thought twins were always alike.

CYNTHIA. We were very much alike in our thoughts. I missed her terribly when she married and went to Singapore. Do you still miss her—or perhaps you'd rather not talk about it ?

SCRAP. I think I *would* like to talk about it. Everyone seems to be frightened of mentioning her.

CYNTHIA. They don't want to upset you.

SCRAP. But it doesn't upset me. It brings her back a bit. That's why I wanted to come to this house—to see the things she used to see. I thought perhaps it would help me to keep her a bit longer.

CYNTHIA (*looking up at* SCRAP). Scrap darling, I'm sure that isn't right. You must try to get over it.

SCRAP. But I have got over it and I don't like being over it. I don't feel miserable any more, you know, but—well, I don't feel *anything* any more and that's rather dull, isn't it ?

CYNTHIA. Is it a sort of empty feeling ?

SCRAP (*after some thought*). Yes, it's exactly that. (*Leaning against the back of* CYNTHIA'S *chair.*) Just meals and lessons and nothing hurting any more. I don't like it. I suppose I sound silly.

CYNTHIA. Not to me. I believe I'm in exactly the same place that you are—a sort of Limbo of the mind. That was stupid of me—you couldn't understand.

SCRAP. But I do know about Limbo. It's in between Heaven and Hell. People there aren't happy and they aren't miserable. They just aren't *anything*. Why, of course, I see—that *is* it.

CYNTHIA. You're very intelligent.

SCRAP. I am in bits. Why are you in Limbo, Auntie Cynthia ?

CYNTHIA. I'm talking a lot of nonsense. Shall we play something ? There used to be some games in that cupboard.

SCRAP (*going and looking in the toy cupboard*). There's Ludo and Halma and Snakes-and-Ladders.

(CYNTHIA *rises and follows her.*)

What happened to all Mummie's dolls ?

CYNTHIA. I don't know, Scrap. Is that a teddy-bear there ?

(SCRAP *brings out an ancient one-armed teddy-bear.*)

(*Taking it.*) Why, it's Symp. (*She comes down* C.)

SCRAP (*following her*). Symp ?

CYNTHIA. We called him that because he was extra sympathetic. We used to hug him whenever we were miserable—when we were in disgrace or the rabbits died or when nobody understood us.

SCRAP. Did Mummie hug him ?

CYNTHIA. We all did. It went on till we were quite big. Hello, Symp, my lad—how did you lose that arm ?

SCRAP. Is he still sympathetic ?

CYNTHIA. He looks it to me. (*She rubs her cheek against his head.*) His fur used to get all sopping with tears. Oh, comfortable Symp. He must be over thirty years old.

(DORA'S *voice calls* " Scrap.")

There's your grannie calling. (*She gives the teddy-bear to* SCRAP *and goes and sits again in the armchair.*)

SCRAP. She does seem to call people rather a lot, doesn't she ? (*She crosses to* CYNTHIA.) Auntie Cynthia—will we ever get out of Limbo ?

CYNTHIA. You will, Scrap. I promise you by everything that ever was.

SCRAP. Then I promise you, too.

(MARGERY *enters from the landing.*)

MARGERY. Scrap dear, your grannie wants——

SCRAP. Yes, I'm coming. (*She puts the teddy-bear on the window-seat.*) Good-bye, Symp.

(*She goes out up* L.)

MARGERY (*down* L. *of the table*). Hello, has old Symp turned up ? Well, I've had a word with Edna.

(CYNTHIA *tidies her work and stands in front of the fire.*)

CYNTHIA. I thought she was lying down with a head.

MARGERY. So she is, but I routed her out. I was quite shocked at Fenny's face at lunch. (*She sits* L. *of the table.*)

CYNTHIA. What did Edna say ?

MARGERY. Oh, all done from the highest motives. Felt it her duty, deeply upset. *She's* gone to bed with aspirin, if you please, while poor wretched Fenny's got to carry on as usual. However, she says Nicholas *doesn't* know, which is something.

CYNTHIA. I must tell Fenny.

MARGERY. I've told her.

CYNTHIA. Was she terribly relieved ?

MARGERY. Well, of course—but she's still pretty nervous. She'll do anything on earth to put him off the scent. I offered her Kenneth and she was very much obliged. And apparently there's a man in the village who's rather keen on her who's coming to-night—a sort of gentleman chicken-farmer.

CYNTHIA. I suppose you'd better give Kenneth a hint.

MARGERY. Oh, I shall tell him to give her a break, but I shan't tell him why. He won't need much encouraging.

(FENNY *enters from the landing.* CYNTHIA *shakes out the dress.*)

Hello, you look better.

FENNY. I've put a little rouge on. And I do feel a bit better. I'll be all right.

CYNTHIA (*going to* FENNY *and giving her the dress*). Here's the dress. That'll be a help. (*She goes back to the fire.*)

FENNY (*up* R.C.). I thought I'd wear my old black.

MARGERY. Pooh, you can't flirt with my husband in your old black. Mind you put rouge on again to-night—it suits you.

CYNTHIA. And I'll give you one of Raquelle's new lipsticks —they're marvellous.

FENNY. You are both being angels. Do you think I'm being terribly weak-minded ? Ought I to rush off and be a typist or something ?

MARGERY. Of course not.

CYNTHIA. You're needed here, Fenny.

FENNY (*stepping down* C.). Oh, I am a bit, aren't I ? And it's the only real home I've ever had. It isn't only Nicholas——

CYNTHIA. You've a perfect right to hang on to what happiness you can.

MARGERY. Is he back from Colchester yet ?

FENNY. Yes, but I dodged him.

(NICHOLAS *calls* " Fenny.")

MARGERY. Pull yourself together now, it's no different from when you saw him last.

(NICHOLAS *enters from the landing.*)

NICHOLAS. There you are. I've brought you some hand lotion. (*He puts the bottle on the table.*)

FENNY. Oh, thanks. As a matter of fact I borrowed some of Gertrude's—but thanks all the same.

(*She suddenly rushes out through the night-nursery.*)

NICHOLAS. There's gratitude for you.

CYNTHIA. She thanked you, didn't she ? What more did you expect for a tuppenny-hapenny bottle of hand lotion ?

NICHOLAS. But damn it, she didn't even take it with her. Oh well—I expect she's overworked. I thought she looked a bit flushed. (*He strolls over to the piano and plays " Pop goes the weasel " with one finger, finally getting stuck for a note.*)

CYNTHIA. D. (*She collects her work-basket and takes it up to the cupboard.*)

NICHOLAS. Thank you. (*He finishes triumphantly.*) There ! And that's all that remains of my musical education.

(*He swings round on the piano-stool.* CYNTHIA *is looking into the cupboard.*)

What are you looking for ?

CYNTHIA. There used to be one little patch of wallpaper that dated back to Father's childhood. That always rather fetched me.

NICHOLAS. Oh, I remember that.

CYNTHIA. I used to love this wallpaper.

MARGERY. It's shockingly faded. Mother ought to have the walls distempered.

CYNTHIA (*looking under the shelf in the cupboard*). Nicholas, do you know what that burn is ?

NICHOLAS. It's where I shut the lighted candle in the cupboard.

(HILDA *comes in from the landing.*)

HILDA. What are you doing ?

(CYNTHIA *sits on the window-seat.*)

MARGERY (*who has settled herself at the table and is doing a jigsaw puzzle*). Enjoying a few moments' well-earned peace.

HILDA. In this house ? I don't believe it. (*She crosses to the fire and sits on the fender.*)

CYNTHIA. There used to be peace here. I remember hours of it on this window-sill. I suppose it was just a personal peace and one spun it round oneself like a cocoon. I honestly have forgotten what peace feels like. (*She opens the window.*)

MARGERY.   I don't know that there's any particular fun about peace.

CYNTHIA.   How exactly the same everything looks from this window. The three elms and the stable clock. It's going to strike.

(*The clock strikes five, a pleasant chime, not over loud.*)

NICHOLAS.   What a devil of a lot of associations one has with that chime.

CYNTHIA.   Will anybody please explain to me why time goes so much faster nowadays ? Is it something to do with the world in general or is it just a sign of middle age ?

NICHOLAS.   Funny—I was talking about that to Fenny last night. There seemed to be hours and hours to spare when we were kids.

MARGERY.   We were probably very bored.

CYNTHIA.   I wasn't. I was always so blooming hopeful. This nursery's rather a harrowing place really. I wish I hadn't such an abominably good memory.

HILDA.   Why ? You had a very happy childhood.

CYNTHIA.   That's why, you goof.

HILDA.   Why didn't you come home sooner, Cynthia ? Of course, I've always imagined you were up to something very peculiar in Paris, but I've never known what.

CYNTHIA.   If you really want to know, Hilda, I have been living with a married man who couldn't get a divorce. I lived with him for six years and now I'm not living with him any more.

HILDA.   Is *that* all ? I imagined far worse. Didn't you, Mar ?

MARGERY.   Well, I thought there might have been several men.

HILDA.   Haven't you been working at Raquelle, then ?

CYNTHIA.   Of course I have. We were jolly hard up. He had to keep a wife and family.

HILDA.   I see. Then it wasn't a life of guilty splendour.

CYNTHIA.   It was not. You knew, didn't you, Nicholas ?

NICHOLAS (*rising to the table*). Yes, Edna heard something. (*He does the puzzle over* MARGERY's *shoulder.*)

CYNTHIA.   She would. Well, now you all know.

HILDA.   I really don't see why that kept you from coming home for seven years.

CYNTHIA.   You know how Mother feels about that sort of thing.

MARGERY.   But you needn't have told her.

CYNTHIA.   She'd have found out. And I should have felt miserable all the time. In this house——

NICHOLAS.   I see what Fatty means.

CYNTHIA.   You know how she talked to us when we grew up.

HILDA. Did she say she'd rather see our coffins lowered down the stairs ?

MARGERY. No. That was Grandma. She had a perfect lust for seeing coffins lowered down the stairs. Mother's not as bad as that. Still, she would have minded.

NICHOLAS. Yes. (*He goes up and leans against the rocking-horse.*) You were perfectly right to keep it dark.

CYNTHIA. And I'm going on keeping it dark. After this week-end I shall just fade away again. If I don't she'll get it out of me. I've been dodging little private chats ever since I arrived.

MARGERY. You seem to be far more shocked at yourself than anyone else is.

CYNTHIA. Mother'd be shocked all right. You know she would, Margery—she'd be absolutely broken up. I happen to be very fond of her.

MARGERY. Well, you know your own business best.

NICHOLAS. I suppose you're right, Fatty, but I'm not quite sure. (*He crosses to* CYNTHIA.) Has it bust up for good ?

CYNTHIA. It has. And I'd rather not talk about it.

HILDA (*sitting in the armchair*). That's a pity, because I'm really very interested. I often think I should like to live with a man myself, just so that he could shut the front door for me at night. I sometimes go back ten times to see if it's really closed.

(NICHOLAS *goes back to the rocking-horse.*)

CYNTHIA. Hilda, this neurotic business of yours is getting past a joke. Are you doing anything about it ?

HILDA. I'm really too busy. If I had time I'd be psycho-analysed. A woman I know says it's probably due to inhibitions, only I don't seem to have any inhibitions, so she thinks there must be something wrong with me. Though in any case, I really haven't got time to rush round having affairs, and of the two evils I think I'd really prefer to go on having a little trouble with front doors and bathroom taps.

NICHOLAS. It doesn't seem to affect your business ability.

HILDA. No. I made over two thousand last year.

NICHOLAS. Great Scot !

HILDA. This woman I know knew a self-made millionaire who had to strike matches to prove to himself he'd turned the electric light off. I should so like to have met him.

NICHOLAS (*leaning on the rocking-horse*). Funny how one's hands remember the feel of things. His right ear was always a bit rough.

CYNTHIA. And the third nail in his mane turned round.

NICHOLAS. So it does.

(*The daylight is fading ; there is a faint glow of sunset outside.*)

CYNTHIA (*gazing out of the window*). I don't like the autumn
any more. I wonder if the rest of you mind growing old as
much as I do ?

MARGERY. You were always so conscious of ages.

HILDA. Yes, Cyn—you used to say they had colours.

CYNTHIA. The teens were green and the twenties yellow ;
the thirties blue and the forties a horrible, horrible brown.

HILDA. I don't really mind being forty.

CYNTHIA. I shall. On my fortieth birthday I shall look in
the glass and say, " It's true, it's happened to you, middle age,
and so will old age and so will death." Only I shan't believe a
word of it.

NICHOLAS. I used to think I should never marry, but I'm
not so sure now.

CYNTHIA. Nicholas, I could strike you. I'm only two years
older than you and already I'm wondering what to do with my
old age—while you're just toying with the idea of making a shot
at married life.

HILDA. With some pretty poppet of eighteen, I suppose.
Men do have the best of things.

NICHOLAS. Not as much as they used to have. Aren't you
piling on the agony a bit, Fatty ? You're still very attractive.
You'll probably marry, yourself.

CYNTHIA. I don't go in for marrying.

NICHOLAS. My dear, you do see yourself as the Scarlet
Woman, don't you ? Have other affairs, then.

CYNTHIA. I don't think middle-aged affairs are very attractive.
What do you think about it all, Marge ?

MARGERY. What all ?

NICHOLAS. Oh, just life, time, change, love and what have
you.

MARGERY. I never can think when I'm doing a jigsaw puzzle.

CYNTHIA. I don't seem to remember you being quite so
bovine, Mar.

MARGERY. Thanks. Well, I'm tolerably happy if it doesn't
annoy you too much.

CYNTHIA. Funny how unalike we three are. I wish to God
Nora hadn't died.

NICHOLAS. I dreamed about Peter last night. He was in his
uniform, looking just as young as Hugh.

HILDA. Well, we may be getting into the sere and yellow,
but at least we are here—which is more than Peter and Nora are.

CYNTHIA. How do you know ?

HILDA. Cynthia, don't—not that I'd mind, really.

(*For a moment they are all quiet in the twilit room. Then* HILDA
moves suddenly.)

Oh !

NICHOLAS. What was it ?

HILDA. Something touched my forehead. A moth or something.

NICHOLAS. Or just " the wind of death's imperishable wing." Who wrote that ?

CYNTHIA (*looking out of the window*). There goes your moth, Hilda.

(BELLE *enters from the landing and comes* c.)

NICHOLAS. Hello, Aunt Belle.

BELLE. Oh, here you all are. I remember coming to tea in this room when I was ten, on your father's birthday.

NICHOLAS. Your ghosts must be quite different from our ghosts. Come and sit down.

(HILDA *moves into the small chair below the fire and* NICHOLAS *puts* BELLE *into the armchair.*)

MARGERY. Did you have a nap ?

(CYNTHIA *shuts the window.*)

BELLE. Well, I lay down. I'm afraid the bed in Little Spare isn't quite what it used to be.

NICHOLAS (*sitting on the fireguard*). Yes it is, Auntie—and so are all the other beds in this house. It's we who have changed. Our bones expect too much.

BELLE. Well, I do like comfort.

NICHOLAS. I hope you enjoyed the bathroom—mahogany round the bath and pictures of the Holy Land. Nothing in this house ever changes.

(CYNTHIA *crosses and sits on the floor below* NICHOLAS.)

CYNTHIA. Except us. Funny to think the last time you saw us we were children.

NICHOLAS. We're all feeling a little broody about the onrush of middle age. (*He puts his hand on* CYNTHIA *and pats her.*) Tell us the secret of age without tears, Auntie.

BELLE. You should ask your mother that—I haven't discovered it. I've always believed in fighting age ; and when I saw your mother last night I decided I'd made a silly old fool of myself.

NICHOLAS. Nonsense, Auntie—you look marvellous.

BELLE. Well, it's been a lot of trouble and I'm not sure that it's been worth it. But I do think that only a very happy woman could dare to trust to Nature as your mother has.

CYNTHIA. But, apart from looks, Aunt Belle, have you minded the *feeling* of growing old ?

BELLE. Yes, my dear. I think it comes hardest on people with good memories.

NICHOLAS. Then you and I are in for it, Fatty.

BELLE. Mind you, you don't feel badly about it all the time. Sometimes you jog on comfortably for months. There *are* things you enjoy more ; food and comfortable beds and books by the fire. I remember once when I was younger than you asking a very old lady about old age, and she said, " Well, my dear, there are always muffins for tea."

CYNTHIA. If one likes muffins.

BELLE. You will, my dear. You'll be surprised what a taste you'll develop for mental muffins. Even I have, and I've taken age harder than most. Of course, you won't like the forties— they're a bit too near to youth ; but the fifties can be quite pleasant—you feel so much younger than the people of sixty. After that even the best memories give you a bit of peace and you only get an occasional stab. Houses bring things back.

CYNTHIA. You must have loathed coming here.

BELLE. In a way I'm loving it, but I'll admit it wasn't only the bed in Little Spare that kept me awake. I keep seeing myself tripping round in a bustle.

NICHOLAS. How pretty you must have looked.

BELLE. I did, my dear—but your mother looked prettier.

(BILL, DORA, SCRAP, FLOUNCY and CHARLES *enter from the landing, in that order. All but* CHARLES *are in outdoor clothes.* BILL *opens the door,* DORA *comes down* R.C., SCRAP *up* C., FLOUNCY *to above the table,* BILL *down* L. CHARLES *shuts the door after* NANNY'S *entrance.*)

DORA. What, all in the dark ?

(*Enter* NANNY *from the night-nursery with a lighted lamp, which she puts on the piano.* NICHOLAS *lights the lamp over the mantel-piece.* NANNY *takes off* BILL'S *coat.* MARGERY *takes off* FLOUNCY'S *coat.* CYNTHIA *goes up to* SCRAP *and takes off her coat.* MARGERY *gives* FLOUNCY'S *coat to* CYNTHIA, *who gives the two coats to* NANNY. BELLE *rises to sit in the chair below the fire.*)

We've been to the village. Just take these for me, will you, dear ?

(*She hands her hat and coat to* HILDA, *who goes out to the landing with them.*)

Come and get warm, Charles.

(*She sits in the armchair.* CHARLES *crosses to the fire.*)

It's turned quite chilly.

CHARLES (*standing with his back to the fire*). There ought to be a good fire in the hall. There ought always to be a good fire

in the hall. I cannot think why, with the house crammed full
of people, no one has time to keep that fire in.

(CYNTHIA *sits on the piano-stool.*)

DORA. Yes, dear, but everyone's been very busy. Really, I
think we might have tea up here as the drawing-room's cleared
for dancing.

BELLE. Nursery tea—that sounds delightful.

DORA. We must count up. Hugh and Laurel are at the
Vicarage. Edna's lying down.

MARGERY. Ken's gone for a tramp.

DORA. Then we're ten. Tell cook, will you, Nanny. I think
we might have muffins.

BILL. I'll tell her.

(NANNY *goes into the night-nursery with the hats and coats.* BILL
runs across and blows down the speaking-tube.)

Tea in the nursery, please—muffins for ten. (*Turning.*) She
was surprised.

NICHOLAS (*behind* DORA's *chair*). Muffins for tea, Aunt Belle.

DORA. Not, of course, that they'll be muffins—one always
says muffins and means crumpets. Come and get warm, Scrap
dear.

(SCRAP *goes to her and sits on the arm of her chair.* BELLE's *arm
is round* BILL.)

Have you been down to the kitchen, Margery?

MARGERY. No, Mother.

DORA. I think perhaps you ought. We don't want cook to
get behind. I do hope the jellies have set.

NICHOLAS (*crossing and sitting on the table*). Mother darling—
no little jobs for anyone. We're going to have a lovely peaceful
tea.

DORA. Very well, dear. (*She pats* SCRAP's *hands.*) Oh, what
cold little hands. Cynthia, you're right out of everything—and
sitting on the piano-stool!

CYNTHIA. I'm quite happy, Mother.

CHARLES. Play something, dear.

BELLE. Do you still sing, Dora? Do you remember the
" Kerry Dance " ?

CHARLES. I don't believe you've sung that for twenty years.

DORA. Oh yes, I have.

BILL. Sing it now, Grannie.

(" Yes do, *etc.,*" *from everyone.*)

DORA. Oh, I couldn't—I've no voice left. Can you play it,
Cynthia ?

CYNTHIA. No, Mother. I'm sure I can't.

MARGERY. Oh, go on, Cyn—you can play anything.

CHARLES. Just try it, dear.

(*Unwillingly,* CYNTHIA *plays while the talk continues. The
"Kerry Dance" is published by Boosey and Hawkes, Ltd.,
295 Regent Street, London, W.1. Before it is sung, the opening
is played twice—the first time about ten bars, the second time about
four bars worked to cue—then introduction and into Song.*)

NICHOLAS. That's it.

SCRAP. Oh—Mummie used to sing this.

DORA. Did she, darling ?

SCRAP. We used to sing it together.

DORA. Then you must sing it with me and help me out with
the high notes.

(*Approval from everyone.*)

Oh no, really I don't think I'd better.

NICHOLAS. Go on, Mother. You can play it all right, Fatty.

(CYNTHIA *stops playing.*)

BILL. Come on, Grannie.

(BILL *pulls her up from her chair.*)

DORA. You mustn't any of you expect too much. Come
along, Scrap dear.

(DORA *crosses to the piano.* CYNTHIA *plays again.* SCRAP
follows DORA *and stands* R. *of her.* FLOUNCY *goes to the window-
seat, takes up the teddy-bear and puts him behind her head.*
MARGERY *helps* NICHOLAS *to pull the table more* C. *She then
takes the jigsaw puzzle and puts it under the rocking-horse.*
CHARLES *sits in the armchair, with* BILL *on the arm.* NICHOLAS
sits on the table, R. *side.* MARGERY *comes and sits on the chair
above the table.*)

Isn't it a bit high, Cynthia ?

(CYNTHIA *stops playing.*)

CYNTHIA. It's in the usual key, Mother.

DORA. Yes, I suppose it is.

(CYNTHIA *starts to play again.* DORA *sings, very quavery on the
high notes, which* SCRAP *takes clearly, though she is too shy to
sing at first.*)

Oh the days of the Kerry dancing !
Oh the ring of the pipers' tune !
Oh for one of those hours of gladness,
Gone—alas—like our youth, too soon.
When the boys begin to gather in the glen of a summer night
And the Kerry pipers tuning made us long with wild delight.
Oh to think of it,
Oh to dream of it,

Fills my heart with tears.
Oh the days of the Kerry dancing !
Oh the ring of the pipers' tune !
Oh for one of those hours of gladness
Gone—alas—like our youth——

(Cʏɴᴛʜɪᴀ *breaks down, near tears.*)

Cʏɴᴛʜɪᴀ. I'm sorry. I can't remember it.
Nɪᴄʜᴏʟᴀs. Oh, go on, Fatty.
Cʏɴᴛʜɪᴀ. I can't, I tell you.
Dᴏʀᴀ. Cynthia, dear——
Nɪᴄʜᴏʟᴀs (*rising*). Don't be so selfish—spoiling Mother's
song like that.
Cʜᴀʀʟᴇs. Try again, my dear.
Cʏɴᴛʜɪᴀ. No, I can't—I won't. (*She bursts into tears.*)

(Dᴏʀᴀ *is terribly upset.*)

Nɪᴄʜᴏʟᴀs (*coming down to below the table*). You ought to be
ashamed of yourself, upsetting Mother like this. A woman of
your age ought to have more control.

(Cʏɴᴛʜɪᴀ *dashes from the room.*)

Sᴄʀᴀᴘ (*to* Nɪᴄʜᴏʟᴀs, *hitting him*). Oh, how could you speak
to her like that !

(Nɪᴄʜᴏʟᴀs *backs to the cupboard.*)

Oh, poor Auntie Cynthia. (*She rushes to the window-seat.*)
Where's Symp ? The teddy-bear——
Fʟᴏᴜɴᴄʏ. I'm using him for a cushion.
Sᴄʀᴀᴘ. Give him to me at once, you beastly Flouncy.

(Sᴄʀᴀᴘ *slaps* Fʟᴏᴜɴᴄʏ, *seizes the teddy-bear and rushes out with
him.* Fʟᴏᴜɴᴄʏ *lets forth a howl.*)

Mᴀʀɢᴇʀʏ (*to* Nɪᴄʜᴏʟᴀs). You ought to be ashamed of yourself. Oh, shut up, Flouncy. Here, come on out.

(*She drags the howling* Fʟᴏᴜɴᴄʏ *out.*)

Nɪᴄʜᴏʟᴀs. Oh, good lord——

(*He dashes out, slamming the door.* Dᴏʀᴀ *moves down stage and
drops her bag.*)

Cʜᴀʀʟᴇs (*rising, crossing to* Dᴏʀᴀ *and picking up her bag*).
Dora, my dear—please don't distress yourself——

(Bɪʟʟ *rises to the fire.*)

Dᴏʀᴀ (*she is trembling*). I oughtn't to have sung. It upset
them. Oh, poor Cynthia—I must go to her——
Cʜᴀʀʟᴇs. Not just yet, dear, you'll only make her worse.
Come and sit down.

(CHARLES *puts* DORA *in the chair* L. *of the table.* BELLE *rises, comes to* R. *of the table and sits.* CHARLES *goes above the table. The lift whistle blows.* BILL *goes to the lift, takes out two dishes of crumpets and puts them on the table.*)

BELLE. It's nothing, Dora. They just got worked up. Better now ? Ah, here's tea.

(GERTRUDE *and* NANNY *enter from the night-nursery with two colossal tea-trays.*)

GERTRUDE. Master Bill, you told cook muffins for ten.
DORA (*hiding her tears*). Our plans have changed a little, Gertrude. I daresay you can manage a few extra, Bill.
BILL. Yes, please.
DORA. Thank you, Gertrude.

(NANNY *and* GERTRUDE *put the trays on the table and exit.* BILL *comes round the top of the table and stands behind* DORA. CHARLES *sits on the chair above the table.*)

BILL. You sang beautifully, Grannie.
DORA. No, dear. I was a conceited old woman to try. I couldn't manage the high notes at all.
BILL. But you put in lots of expression.
DORA. Thank you, Bill. Tell your Aunt Hilda the tea's in. (*She pours out.*)

(BILL *goes out.*)

I do apologize.
BELLE. Why, Dora——
DORA. They're all so upset.
CHARLES. They'll be all right, my dear. Ah! Nursery tea. (*Offering the muffins.*) Muffins, Belle ?

(BELLE *takes one.*)

The three old people, all trying to hide their distress, settle to their muffins round the nursery table as—

The CURTAIN *falls.*

SCENE 3

SCENE.—*The Nursery. Late evening. The fire burns brightly ; only the lamp over the mantelpiece is alight. From below comes the sound of dance music, played on a piano and violin. The music played is " Thanks for the Memory," once through. The first eight bars loudly before the* CURTAIN *rises.*

When the CURTAIN *rises,* HUGH *is sitting on the arm of the armchair, smoking.* LAUREL *comes in from the night-nursery.*

LAUREL. He's just dropping off. She's simply marvollous with him. (*She goes over to* HUGH, *who rises.*)

(NANNY *comes from the night-nursery and goes to the table, where she has been running ribbon in a baby's frock.*)

HUGH. I wish we had you always, Nanny.

NANNY. So do I, Mr. Hugh. I've been like a dog with two tails all this week-end.

HUGH. We couldn't afford you—even if Grannie could spare you.

LAUREL. It is a shame. You're wasted here with no babies to handle.

NANNY. You'd think maybe I'd have lost the knack after all these years of house-work—but it comes back. I always had a way with babies. Even when I was fifteen I could manage them better than old Nanny who was here—not that she'd admit it. (*She looks back into the night-nursery.*) I think I'll just sit by him till he's right off.

(*She goes in, taking the work-basket and frock with her.*)

LAUREL. Bless you, Nanny dear. (*She goes to the window.*)

(EDNA *enters from the landing, leaving the door open. She comes to above the table.*)

HUGH. Hello, Mother.

EDNA. Have you seen Nicholas anywhere ?

LAUREL. Not for an hour or so. He was hunting for Fenny—I think she'd cut a dance or something.

(*End of dance music. There is talking and clapping under the stage.*)

HUGH. I must say I thought she was behaving a bit oddly, didn't you, Mother ?—Giggling and romping.

EDNA. Poor girl.

HUGH. Why poor ? She seemed to be enjoying herself. I wonder if she's had a drop too much champagne. What a lark !

EDNA. Don't be so incredibly vulgar, Hugh.

HUGH. Well, really, darling——!

EDNA (*going up to the door*). I'm sorry. I'm tired. I'm going to bed. Good night.

(*She goes, leaving the door open.*)

HUGH. Tut, tut, something wrong there.

LAUREL. Ought I to go after her ?

HUGH. Lord, no—she hates being fussed over. Shall we go down and dance again ?

LAUREL. Yes, lets.

(KENNETH *and* FENNY *enter.*)

Oh, hello.

KENNETH. Fenny's feeling a bit done up—thought it might be quiet up here.

LAUREL (*stepping to* FENNY). Anything I can do ?

FENNY (*going to the window-seat and sitting*). No, thanks—I'm quite all right really.

HUGH. Well, don't make a row or you'll wake our offspring. (*He goes up to the door, slapping* KENNETH *on the back in passing.*) Come on.

(HUGH *and* LAUREL *go off.*)

KENNETH. Here, put your feet up. (*He sits beside her and puts her feet on his lap.*) I say, what jolly little shoes. You're a bit of a Cinderella, you know, turning up at the ball and cutting everyone else out. There—now you've lost your slipper. (*He takes her slipper.*)

FENNY. That's where the resemblance ends.

KENNETH. Oh, I dunno. I'm going to hang about at midnight, anyhow.

FENNY. What for ?

KENNETH. Didn't all her clothes fall off ?

FENNY. No, they just turned to rags. And next day she was back in the kitchen.

KENNETH. Ah, but then the prince rolled along.

FENNY. I wonder if he kept chickens.

KENNETH. What ? Oh, you mean that chap with the bald head you were carrying on with. I say, you haven't half been going it to-night—I never saw such a change in a girl.

FENNY. You've been a bit of a surprise yourself.

KENNETH. What, because I kissed you ? You didn't mind, did you ?

FENNY. Oh no. Did Margery tell you to ?

KENNETH. Good God, no. What an extraordinary thing to say.

FENNY. Didn't she tell you to be nice to me ?

KENNETH. Well, she did tell me to dance with you a bit, but the rest has been entirely my own initiative. I say, you won't tell, will you ?

FENNY. I promise.

KENNETH. Good girl. (*He tickles her foot.*)

FENNY. Don't, Ken. (*She giggles.*) No—for goodness' sake——

(*She tries to pull her feet away, but* KENNETH *holds them.* NICH-OLAS *enters in the middle of the struggle and comes above the table.*)

NICHOLAS. Sorry if I'm interrupting.

(FENNY *escapes.*)

KENNETH. Not at all, old man. (*He rises to down* o. *and holds up the shoe.*) Who's the owner of this pretty thing ?

c

FENNY. Give it to me, Kenneth. (*She follows* KENNETH *down* C.)

KENNETH. Oh no. (*He kneels to put it on.*)

NICHOLAS (*now down* L.—*to* FENNY). I hate to seem fussy, but you've cut four dances with me.

FENNY. I'm sorry. I lost my programme.

KENNETH. No, you didn't, old dear, I've got it. (*He takes it from his pocket.*)

FENNY. That's the worst of these silly programmes—one doesn't memorize.

NICHOLAS. One usually has a vague consciousness of four dances together, including supper.

KENNETH (*reading the programme*). There we are, large as life. My fault, old man. We haven't been bothering much with programmes.

NICHOLAS (*going to the piano-stool*). It's of supreme unimportance.

FENNY (*desperately*). Oh, do get up, Ken, I'll fasten it.

(*She fastens her shoe.* KENNETH *rises and turns to* NICHOLAS.)

KENNETH. Shall I hand her over now ?

FENNY. I can't dance any more, I'm too hot.

NICHOLAS. You look as if you were going to have apoplexy.

KENNETH. I say, that's damned rude.

(CYNTHIA *enters from the night-nursery with a book.*)

CYNTHIA. Shut up here, can't you—you'll wake the infant.

FENNY. I'll just go and put some powder on.

(*She goes out.*)

KENNETH. The poor kid put a bit of make-up on and then got a natural flush.

NICHOLAS. How very interesting.

KENNETH. Sorry about the dances.

NICHOLAS. Oh, don't be ridiculous. Margery was looking for you.

KENNETH. Oh, was she ? Suppose I'd better go and report. Thanks.

(*He goes out, whistling.*)

CYNTHIA. I've been reading to the kids. It's hopeless to expect them to sleep with a dance in the house.

NICHOLAS (*crossing in front of the table to* R.C.). And what a dance—half the village seems to be here. (*He turns to* CYNTHIA, *who sits on the table.*) I say, did you notice Fenny ?

CYNTHIA. I thought she looked very pretty.

NICHOLAS. She always looks quite pretty. Good lord, I

think she must have gone a bit dotty to-night. (*Going to the fire.*)
She danced six times running with that frightful chicken farmer.

CYNTHIA. There's no law against it.

NICHOLAS. But you should have seen her—giggling and
flirting. And just now, with Kenneth——

CYNTHIA. She doesn't get many parties. I don't blame her
for enjoying herself.

NICHOLAS (*sitting in the armchair*). Oh well, I suppose the
poor little devil doesn't know any better. Funny, I could have
sworn she had a natural dignity.

CYNTHIA (*after a second's pause—rising*). Nicholas, do you
like Fenny ?

NICHOLAS. Of course I like her—that's why it's rather painful
to see her making an ass of herself. Don't we all like her ?
She's a family institution.

CYNTHIA. Yes, I see. (*Giving it up.*) I think we ought to
go down.

NICHOLAS. I suppose so. (*He rises to the table.*) I say,
Fatty—sorry about this afternoon.

CYNTHIA. My fault. Served me right. (*Turning away to the
piano.*) But I just couldn't stand it—that song and Mother's
voice breaking and poor Nora's child. (*She turns to him.*) You
felt exactly the same, didn't you ?

NICHOLAS. Yes. That's why I barked at you.

CYNTHIA. Between the two of us we upset Mother pretty
badly.

NICHOLAS. My dear, she'd completely recovered half an hour
after when I apologized. Mother has an invincible happiness.

CYNTHIA. Lord, I wish I'd never come. Her eyes follow me
about asking questions.

NICHOLAS. Why don't you have it out with her ? (*He crosses
to her.*)

CYNTHIA. I'd die of embarrassment. Oh, you know it
wouldn't work. I'll just slink away again.

(CHARLES *enters with* BELLE, *who is beautifully dressed, but in a
frock that makes no concessions to old age. They leave the door
open.*)

BELLE. Why aren't you young things dancing ?

CYNTHIA. Feeling rather mature, Auntie.

BELLE. Nonsense. We had a turn ourselves, didn't we,
Charles ?

(CHARLES *crosses to the armchair and puts* BELLE *in it.*)

CHARLES. And now we're going to indulge in a little sitting out.

(*The* " *Blue Danube* " *is heard from below. A hundred and
twenty-eight bars are played.*)

Ah, " The Beautiful Blue Danube."

NICHOLAS.   Do you remember the dancing-class, Fatty ?

CYNTHIA.   Fan, mittens and bronze sandals—and you boys skulking in a corner.

NICHOLAS.   Come on, we'll show them.

(NICHOLAS *and* CYNTHIA *go off*.)

CHARLES (*standing by* BELLE).   They played it at our dancing-class, too.

BELLE.   And at the dance your mother gave for us bridesmaids, the night of your wedding.

CHARLES.   Ah, I missed that.   I rather think I was on the English Channel, thanking God I'd married a good sailor.

BELLE.   That was the night I accepted your brother William—there didn't seem to be any point in going on refusing him.   Did you know about me then, Charles, or not till afterwards ?

CHARLES.   I think I always knew.

BELLE.   You know, there's something rather luxurious in being able to sit back and tell a man you've been in love with him for fifty years.   I guess I'm entitled to some sort of Golden Anniversary myself.

CHARLES.   My dear Belle.

BELLE.   You've never written your book, Charles—or gone into Parliament.   All the things you planned as a boy——

CHARLES.   I've never done any of them.

BELLE.   You would have done if you'd married me.

CHARLES.   I wonder.   You women are much too fond of fancying you can make geniuses of men.   And anyway, there are far too many books written and far, far too many people in Parliament.

BELLE.   Don't pretend, Charles.   You had great gifts.

CHARLES.   Not really, Belle.   You see, when I came to have a little leisure to explore the minds of other men, I found that everything I wanted to say had been said by someone else.   I was always expecting to get some epoch-making new idea, but I never did.   I think I might have had a shot at politics—but there were so many far more important things to do.

BELLE.   What things ?

(*The dance music stops. Talk and clapping can be heard.*)

CHARLES.   Surely you have realized that any house that contains Dora also contains a number of Little Jobs ?   You would be surprised, for instance, what a very large number of shelves I have put up and an almost equally large number I have taken down.   (*He walks down* c.)   Then there have been children to play with, dogs to take walks, gardens to plan, neighbours to visit——

BELLE.   And you call these things important ?

CHARLES. I do indeed. I call the sum-total of any man's happiness important.

BELLE. Have you been happy, Charles ?

CHARLES. So happy that I am sometimes tempted to erect a statue to myself. I should like people to be reminded that happiness isn't quite obsolete. (*He goes back to* BELLE.) Have you been happy, Belle ?

BELLE. That's rather a cruel question.

CHARLES. Nonsense. Confess now—you haven't given me a thought for years.

BELLE. I've thought of you every day of my life. I'm not ashamed to own it.

CHARLES. You never did have a proper sense of shame. (*He goes to the table and sits on it.*) You were a baggage at seven and you're a baggage at seventy.

BELLE. Do you really think that——? Did you think it thirty years ago, after William died ?

CHARLES. I'd certainly every cause to. You came very near to breaking up this happy home, you know.

BELLE. No—never that.

CHARLES. Then shall we say, to putting rather a blot on the escutcheon ?

BELLE. But I didn't manage it.

CHARLES (*chuckling*). No, you didn't manage it.

BELLE. Don't gloat so. You were always cruel to me.

CHARLES. Because you were a challenge and a menace and always will be.

(BELLE *takes out her handkerchief.* CHARLES *goes over to her quickly.*)

Why, my dear, I was teasing you.

BELLE. I find one's never too old to be hurt.

CHARLES. God bless my soul, you preposterous woman—two husbands and Lord knows how many side-lines, and just because one poor country lout managed to resist you—— (*Going up towards the door.*) No, I won't sentimentalize with you. What you need's a stiff whisky. Come on.

(DORA *enters to* c., *looking exquisite in a silver picture frock.*)

DORA. Oh, here you are. Why, Belle, dear——

CHARLES. We've been talking over old times. Poor William, you know——

DORA. Of course. Poor William. And your American husband—what was his name ?

BELLE. Elmer.

DORA. Poor Elmer. How I wish they could both be here. Though I suppose that wouldn't be quite practicable. Get her a good strong drink, Charles.

CHARLES. I was just suggesting it.

DORA. I'll be with you in a minute, dear—I just want **a word** with Nanny.

(*She goes into the night-nursery.*)

BELLE (*rising*). I'm a silly old woman.

CHARLES (*coming down to face her*). That's the first time I've ever seen you cry.

BELLE. And it'll be the last. Lead me to that whisky.

(CHARLES *escorts her out.* DORA *returns, followed by* NANNY· *The dance band starts to play waltzes. "Stories from the Vienna Woods"—Strauss. Eighty-two bars are played and seque into "Die Fledermaus" waltz. Forty-eight bars are played.* DORA *crosses above the table to* R.C. NANNY *comes down* L. *of the table.*)

DORA. Are they all asleep ?

NANNY. Miss Scrap is. The other two are beyond human control. They've gone down to get some more supper out of cook.

DORA. Good gracious. Well, it's a very special occasion. You'd better make the fire up in case any of them are ill in the night.

(NANNY *crosses to the fire and puts coal on.*)

Not finding it too much for you, are you ?

NANNY. Indeed no, ma'am. It's a great pleasure. It's been like old times in the nursery.

DORA. How long have you been with us, Nanny ?

NANNY. Forty-seven years, ma'am. I came as nursemaid when Mr. Peter was six months old. He was the best baby of them all—and his little grandson's just like him.

DORA. My dear Peter.

NANNY. We shall see him again, ma'am.

DORA. Of course we shall.

NANNY. I've been thinking of him a lot this evening. And I keep on remembering you in that blue dressing-gown with the little white bows, whisking in and out like you used to at night when any of them were ill, with your pretty fair hair down your back.

DORA. Fancy your remembering that. What a long time we've been friends, Nanny. And now you must go to bed, because baby'll wake you early.

NANNY. Good night, ma'am.

DORA. Good night, Nanny, and thank you for all these years. (*She pats* NANNY'S *hand.*) Sleep well.

(NANNY *crosses below the table and goes into the night-nursery.* DORA *goes to the mirror and arranges her hair.* CHARLES *returns. The band is now playing the waltz from "Die Fleder-maus."*)

Is she all right now ?

CHARLES (*crossing to above the armchair*). She's doing up her face.

DORA. Poor Belle—she's as much in love with you as ever. At her age !

CHARLES (*chuckling*). Aren't you in love with me ?

DORA. I hope I don't make eyes at you. (*She listens, crossing to above the table.*) That must be the last dance.

(*The dance band stops.*)

I told them to play those old waltzes at the end. People like them.

CHARLES. Did you notice Fenny to-night ?

DORA. Mark my words—that chicken farmer is going to propose.

CHARLES. Good lord—she wouldn't accept him ?

DORA. Well, he isn't nearly good enough for her, but every woman likes to marry. You could lend him a little capital. Charles—

(*He goes to her.*)

—I haven't spoken to Cynthia yet—a whole day wasted. I must tackle it to-morrow.

(*The stable clock begins to strike twelve.*)

CHARLES. It's to-morrow now. Our Golden Wedding day.

DORA. Many, many congratulations, my dear. (*She kisses him.*)

CHARLES. And to you, my love.

DORA. Now we must go down. They'll be playing " Sir Roger " at the end.

CHARLES. We shall hear it when it starts. I do hope my legs'll be equal to it. Let's sit quiet a bit.

(*He puts the armchair in the firelight for* DORA, *then takes the chair from* R. *of the table and puts it* L. *of* DORA'S.)

DORA. Very well.

(*They sit by the fire.*)

Our Golden Wedding. What do we have next ? A Diamond Wedding ? I'm sure we shall both live to be very old. Charles——

CHARLES. Yes, Dora ?

DORA. It isn't really the right moment now—but, something that Nanny was saying——

CHARLES. Yes, my dear ?

DORA. It's something we haven't discussed for years. Has religion ever got—any clearer to you ?

CHARLES. No, my dear, I don't think it has.

DORA. I was afraid not. I did so hope that if I prayed about it and didn't worry you, but just took you to church every Sunday. Don't you believe there's *anything* after life ?

CHARLES. No, my dear. I'm just as I always was—no, that's not quite true. I used to be *sure* there was nothing, and now, well, I'm not quite sure of anything.

DORA. Oh, but that's a very definite improvement. You used to be an atheist and now you're an agnostic. I think that's splendid.

CHARLES (*laughing*). You are an extraordinary woman. After fifty years you still manage to astonish me.

DORA. Why ?

CHARLES. You're so matter of fact. But I can't tell you how relieved I am—you used to be so distressed about it.

DORA. I used to be afraid that God might punish you. But I see now that with such a good man it could only be a question of His explaining to you. Of course, I do wish you believed, because you'd feel so much more comfortable, wouldn't you ?

CHARLES. Yes, Dora. I'd like to go on.

DORA. You will, my dear. You see, the fact that you don't believe in Heaven can't make it not there, can it ? There are some very good modern books about religion. Shall I send for some ?

CHARLES. Are *you* quite sure about Heaven, Dora ?

DORA. Utterly and completely sure, Charles.

CHARLES. Then I find that more convincing than all the books that were ever written. You see, my dear, in all our discussions for the last fifty years, you have invariably been right.

(" *Sir Roger de Coverley* " *is heard from below.* CHARLES *rises and puts his chair back at the table.*)

They're playing " Sir Roger " ; we must go down.

DORA (*rising*). It's been a good party, I think. Nothing spectacular, but very pleasant. (*She is shaking out her silk skirt with a charming grace.*)

CHARLES. Very pleasant indeed.

DORA. Well, now it's over. (*She turns out the lamp over the mantelpiece.*)

CHARLES. Not quite, my love.

(DORA *goes to* CHARLES *up* C.)

(*He suddenly laughs.*) That's my earliest memory—the pattern of the fireguard on the nursery ceiling.

The guests below start to clap in time to the music, which grows louder. Voices are heard calling, " Grannie, Grandpa, Mother, Father, Mrs. Randolph," etc. DORA *and* CHARLES *go out and—*

The CURTAIN *falls.*

ACT III

SCENE 1

SCENE.—*The Dining-room. Sunday evening about half-past six.
The room is heavily Victorian with dark red walls hung with
rather mediocre family portraits, none earlier than 1850, but,
like every other room in the house, it possesses a certain charm,
though one would be hard put to it to say why.*

There is a sideboard R. *with a door above it. On the extreme*
R. *of the back wall is a large built-in cupboard for glass, etc.,
then comes the fireplace and then the double doors leading to
the hall. When these are open the hall and front door can be
seen. On the* L. *are two long windows. A large mahogany
table takes up most of the centre of the room. There are silver
candelabra on the mantelpiece, but at present the room is lit
by lamps.*

*(See Photograph of Scene ; also Ground Plan at end of play
for positions at table.)*

When the CURTAIN *rises,* MARGERY *is standing on a chair handing
down glasses from the top shelf of the cupboard to* CYNTHIA.
HILDA *is laying silver on the table. She has a basket of cutlery,
and she starts laying* MARGERY'S *place.* EDNA, *a woolly cardigan
over her evening dress, is sitting by the fire. The others have
not yet changed into evening dress.*

CYNTHIA (*taking three glasses to the table*). Do we need the
large glasses ?
MARGERY. Better put them out, Mother likes plenty of glass.
HILDA. I do so loathe this job. Gertrude could do it in half
the time.

(CYNTHIA *fetches three more glasses.*)

MARGERY. We always have laid the table for family parties
and we always shall. It's a sort of rite.
HILDA. We're supposed to have an artistic touch.
EDNA. Why don't we go on strike ?
HILDA (*laying* CHARLES'S *place*). One doesn't go on strike
against Mother. I don't know why, but one just doesn't. I
can't say you're doing an awful lot.
EDNA. I'm so cold.

73

(CYNTHIA *fetches three more glasses.*)

And I never can remember your mother's fads about table-laying. It's a miracle to me she ever gave up damask table-cloths.

MARGERY. Fenny got her out of that.

EDNA. Have any of you talked to Fenny to-day ? She's avoiding me.

CYNTHIA (*fetching three more glasses*). She's avoiding the whole world as much as possible and just getting on with her job.

EDNA. It may turn out all for the best if this chicken farmer really is keen on her——

CYNTHIA. He's a horror. You can't get her off your conscience like that.

EDNA. I resent that. I acted from the very highest motives.

CYNTHIA (*fetching three more glasses*). That's nice for you, of course, but it doesn't improve matters for Fenny. (*Counting up the glasses.*) That's the lot, Marge.

EDNA. I don't think I shall come down at Christmas.

(HILDA *moves the basket to* L. *end of the table and lays* BELLE'S *place.*)

HILDA. I don't know why you ever come. You know you loathe our family parties.

EDNA. I got into the habit when Hugh was small.

MARGERY. I don't see how you could very well help coming —considering the whacking big allowance Father gives you.

(EDNA *gives her a quick glance of annoyance.*)

Fruit plates.

(*She hands them down.* CYNTHIA *puts them on the sideboard.*)

EDNA. Well, I think I shall cry off at Christmas and Nicholas ought to, too.

HILDA. Why ?

EDNA. On Fenny's account. He'd better come away with me.

CYNTHIA (*turning on* EDNA). Well, I'm damned.

(MARGERY *gets off her chair, comes to the table and dusts the glasses. She leaves the cupboard doors open.*)

MARGERY. The way you put Nicholas in your pocket's absolutely sickening.

HILDA. I quite agree. We know he won't marry Fenny, but the way you've got your claws into him, he'll never marry anyone.

EDNA. How dare you speak to me like that !

HILDA. I shall speak to you any way I like, and if you're

not going to do any work for goodness' sake get out of the way. (*She tips* EDNA *out of her chair and moves the chair nearer the fire.*) We're laying the table.

EDNA. I've told you I'm frozen. Oh, very well. (*She crosses and sits in a chair by the window down* L., *pulling her woolly coat round herself for warmth.*) Now perhaps you'll go on with this concerted attack.

(CYNTHIA *comes below the table and puts glasses at places, going from* R. *to* L.)

CYNTHIA. You won't deny you've made the week-end pretty embarrassing.

MARGERY. And if you ask me, with no real reason. Fenny wouldn't have made a fool of herself.

HILDA. You've been an interfering busybody.

EDNA. This is a conspiracy.

MARGERY. It certainly will be if you try to keep Nicholas away from home.

CYNTHIA. It would break Mother's heart. (*She puts a glass at* CHARLES'S *place.*)

EDNA. You haven't been very fussy about her heart. You haven't been home for seven years.

CYNTHIA (*picking up another glass and turning on* EDNA). How dare you !

(HILDA *picks up a carving-knife and steel.* GERTRUDE *enters with a pile of napkins.*)

GERTRUDE. There's the napkins (*she puts them on the sideboard*) and the mistress says will you please make them into water-lilies.

(*They all wait till the door closes ; then rush back to the quarrel.*)

HILDA. You will apologize for that last remark to Cynthia.

(MARGERY *takes the basket and puts it in the sideboard cupboard. She then returns to the table and sets glasses along the upstage side. She brings the bottle of almonds with her.*)

EDNA. I shall apologize for nothing. And if this argument is to continue you will kindly put that carving-knife down. You're too neurotic to be trusted with it.

HILDA. I may be neurotic, but I've never cradle-snatched my brother-in-law. (*She sharpens the carver.*)

CYNTHIA. Oh, chuck it, Hilda.

(HILDA *puts down the carver.*)

You're perfectly right, Edna. I have not been home for seven years and, as you make a point of knowing everyone's business,

C**

you probably know why. (*She lays glasses for* HILDA *and* BELLE.)
It was most graceful and charming of you to bring it up.

EDNA. I oughtn't to have said it. I'm sorry, Cynthia.

CYNTHIA. That's all right, Edna. (*She goes to the sideboard, takes a chocolate-box and two silver dishes to the upstage* R. *corner of the table and puts out chocolates.*)

HILDA (*pointing the steel at* EDNA). Well, it's not all right for me. Before this argument closes there's something I should like you to know, Edna. I didn't like you when Peter married you, I haven't liked you during twenty-five years and I don't like you now. (*She crosses to the sideboard cupboard.*)

EDNA (*rising to* MARGERY). Are those your sentiments too ?

MARGERY. Of course not. And they're not Hilda's really. Do you want to walk out with dignity or could you bring yourself to put out the salted almonds ?

(HILDA *takes out two cruets from the downstage cupboard.*)

EDNA. I'm much too upset. I've done nothing whatever to warrant this attack. I've said I was sorry to Cynthia and you all know I was perfectly sincere in my attitude to Fenny. And if you wanted to hurt me, Hilda, you've certainly succeeded.

(*She goes out up* L. MARGERY *puts out the almonds.*)

CYNTHIA. You'll have to apologize.

HILDA. I shall not. (*She shuts the cupboard door, then opens it again and digs inside with the steel.*)

MARGERY. Oh, for goodness' sake let's get the table finished. What are you doing, Hilda ?

HILDA (*on her knees, peering into the sideboard cupboard*). I thought I might have shut a fly in. (*She shuts the cupboard.*)

MARGERY. Batty. These flowers aren't up to much.

CYNTHIA. Everyone seems to have sent great tall things in pots.

(HILDA *rises with the two cruets, one in each hand, and the steel under her arm.*)

Do we still have the epergne ? (*She goes up to the glass-cupboard.*)

MARGERY. We don't at Christmas because we have the reindeer and the cake. Do we have the epergne, Hilda ?

HILDA (*putting one cruet at* R. *end of the table*). Yes—no. I haven't the faintest idea.

CYNTHIA. Mother's sure to want it. (*She brings the epergne from the cupboard.*)

(MARGERY *moves the vase from* O. *of the table to* R. *end.*)

What a little darling. Anyone who does this with asters deserves a medal. (*She gets a jug of water from the sideboard and starts to arranae flowers.*)

HILDA (*placing the other cruet and the steel at* L. *end of the table*).
This mustard isn't fresh.

MARGERY (*placing the chocolate dishes*).   It'll do—it's getting
so late.

(BELLE *enters from the hall.* HILDA *sits on the downstage arm of*
CHARLES'S *chair.*)

Hullo, Auntie.

BELLE (*standing* C. *above the table*).   Well, this is a great
occasion. I came here to your great-grandfather's Golden
Wedding when I was a girl.

CYNTHIA.   Did you, Auntie ?

BELLE.   Such an enormous meal, and the speeches——   Your
father always spoke so well.

MARGERY.   Father hasn't made a speech for donkey's years.
Nicholas always does them now.

HILDA.   Will he do Grand Toast to-night ?

MARGERY.   I expect so. (*To* BELLE.)   He always does it at
Christmas—it's a sort of special toast to us all en masse. He
does it rather well.

HILDA.   Will you come down at Christmas ?

BELLE.   No, my dear. This house is a bit too much for me.

CYNTHIA.   Poor Auntie.

BELLE.   Oh, I'm all right. I guess I'll just trot off to the
South of France for a few months.   I'm too old a hand at fighting
age to have lost my technique. But I won't come here again.
You can't play ostriches with time in this house. What a silly,
vain old woman you must think me.

(*She goes up* L. *to the door.* HILDA *rises to behind the chair.*)

MARGERY.   Of course not.

BELLE.   One just must *not* remember things. You take that
to heart, all of you. Now for a bit of extra war-paint.

(*She goes out into the hall.*)

MARGERY.   Poor old dear, she does hate being old. (*She
goes up* R. *to the cupboard with the empty almond bottle and chocolate-
box.*)

CYNTHIA.   It's queer, that. Yesterday she seemed to have
quite a bit of philosophy.

(HILDA *moves to the door.*)

MARGERY.   Here, where are you going ?

HILDA.   To make it up with Edna. I don't seem to have
any capacity for sustained rage these days. Still, it was good
while it lasted.

(*She goes out into the hall.*)

CYNTHIA (*now seated above the table struggling with the epergne*). This poor brute's simply screaming for carnations and gypsophila.

(KENNETH *enters up* R.)

KENNETH. Any chance of a drink anywhere ? There's nothing in the pantry.

MARGERY (*shutting the cupboard*). You'll have to wait till Father comes down.

KENNETH (*crossing to* L.). I wonder if Fenny can fix me something.

MARGERY. Here, you lay off Fenny for a bit.

KENNETH. Good lord, you asked me to give her a break.

MARGERY. Well, you overdid it.

KENNETH (*cheerfully*). I suppose someone saw me kissing her on the kitchen stairs. (*He flops into* CHARLES'S *chair.*)

MARGERY. Kenneth, you ought to be ashamed of yourself. And you've got the nerve to tell me !

KENNETH. When I give a girl a break, I *give* her a break.

MARGERY. Oh, don't sit there looking complacent. Go and dress.

(*Voices are heard in the hall.*)

There are the children.

(NANNY, FLOUNCY, SCRAP *and* BILL, *all in outdoor clothes, enter from the hall.* BILL *and* FLOUNCY *open the doors and enter first, then* SCRAP, *who crosses to* CYNTHIA, *and lastly* NANNY. BILL *goes to* MARGERY ; FLOUNCY *sits on the arm of* CHARLES'S *chair* ; NANNY *remains standing two steps down from the door.*)

Did you have a good time ?

FLOUNCY. Lovely, Mummie. She showed us the secret passage and Bill crawled right inside.

BILL. Shut up, Flouncy. I did it—I tell it.

FLOUNCY. Oh, you're such a baby about telling things.

NANNY. Her ladyship sent these from the hothouses.

(*She steps down with orchids.* MARGERY *takes them and puts them on the table.*)

MARGERY. Oh, corn in Egypt. Look, Cynthia—just right for the table.

CYNTHIA. Oh, I *can't* do this all over again. (*Rising and holding up the epergne.*) How does it look ?

BILL. Jolly funny, Auntie Cyn.

CYNTHIA. It isn't meant to look funny.

SCRAP. I think it looks splendid.

CYNTHIA. Thank you, Scrap.

BILL. Where are the crackers ?

MARGERY. There aren't any. It isn't Christmas.

BILL. No crackers ? Pooh, what a rotten party.

(*He takes a chocolate.* MARGERY *takes it from him and puts it back.*)

MARGERY. Now run along and get dressed. (*To* NANNY.) I'll be up to give them a last look over.

SCRAP. Will you come and give me a last look over, Auntie Cynthia ?

CYNTHIA. I will, darling.

(DORA *enters* R., *looking lovely as usual.*)

DORA. What ! Not dressed yet ?

(SCRAP *steps back.* KENNETH *and* FLOUNCY *rise.*)

FLOUNCY. Look what Lady Ridgewell sent.

(MARGERY *indicates the orchids.*)

DORA. How very nice of her. I was wondering what we could use for the table. Good gracious, what are you doing with that dreadful old epergne ? We haven't used it for years.

CYNTHIA. Oh, Mother—and I've been simply wrestling with it.

DORA. Put it away, dear, and we'll have the cut-glass bowl instead.

(CYNTHIA *puts the epergne on the sideboard.* DORA *gets the glass bowl and arranges the orchids in it.* SCRAP *goes up to join* NANNY.)

FLOUNCY. Grannie, Bill got on the pony and he rode right round the paddock and——

(CYNTHIA *helps* DORA *with the orchids.*)

BILL. You've done it again, Flouncy. I rode it—I tell it. Mummie, will you speak to her—she's always telling my things.

MARGERY (*to* FLOUNCY). You know he likes to tell things.

BILL. Next time you do it, I'll lam you.

(*He shakes his fist at* FLOUNCY. MARGERY *catches his arm.*)

DORA. Hush, dear, that's no way to speak. Now off you go to dress.

(NANNY, FLOUNCY *and* SCRAP *go into the hall, followed by* KENNETH, *who first puts his chair in to the table.* MARGERY *is just taking* BILL *off when* DORA *recalls them.*)

Just one minute, Margery ; can you absolutely guarantee that when your father says grace to-night, that child will not say " Selfridge's " ?

MARGERY. What about it, Bill ?

BILL. I'll do my very best, Grannie, but it sort of comes over me.

(MARGERY *and* BILL *go, closing the door.*)

DORA (*laughing as she puts the orchid bowl in the c. of the table*). Really. We really oughtn't to laugh at him.

CYNTHIA (*taking the orchid basket and duster and putting them in the sideboard cupboard*). I don't think there's much more I can do.

DORA. The napkins, dear.

CYNTHIA. I never could do water-lilies.

DORA (*moving the chair from R. of the fire to the table near R. end*). Then I'll do them and you shall sit and talk to me.

CYNTHIA (*getting the napkins from the sideboard*). I ought to be dressing.

DORA. There's plenty of time yet. This is the last chance of a chat we shall have—if you really insist on going to-morrow ?

CYNTHIA. I'm afraid I must.

DORA. Put them here, dear.

(CYNTHIA *puts the napkins near* DORA, *who sits.*)

Now sit down, darling.

(*Unwillingly* CYNTHIA *sits in* DORA'S *armchair at* R. *end of the table.*)

You know, you need a holiday. You're looking tired.

CYNTHIA. Not really ; just old, I expect.

DORA. Nonsense, you're a young woman. (*She starts doing a water-lily.*)

CYNTHIA. I'm thirty-seven.

DORA. I think that's a charming age. Don't waste it, my dear.

CYNTHIA. Waste it ?

DORA. No one ever seems to like the age they are. Flouncy wants to be grown-up and Belle's still pining for her youth. Poor Belle, she's so determined to forget her age that she never stops remembering it. That's not the way to keep young.

CYNTHIA. Then what is ? You've never minded growing old.

DORA. No, I can honestly say I've enjoyed all my ages, and I know your father has. I think, perhaps, it's a question of being interested in life. There are so many things—people, theatres, books, wireless. We've a new puppy arriving next week—really one life isn't long enough. Your father always says he'd like to be the Wandering Jew—provided, of course, that I was a Wandering Jewess. I don't think we shall ever be bored even if we live to be quite old.

CYNTHIA. What would you call quite old, darling ?

DORA. Oh, eighty-five or ninety. Of course, when one reads

in a book about a woman of seventy, *she* seems old, but it's different when it's yourself.

CYNTHIA. You always do seem just middle-aged to me.

DORA. Your father says middle age is stretching out, just as youth is. One's young till one's forty and middle-aged till one's eighty. I daresay by the time *you're* old we shall have got rid of old age altogether. Anyway, there are nice things about every age if people realize it in time instead of in retrospect. You should try to be your age and enjoy being it, my dear.

CYNTHIA. I've never heard you philosophize before.

DORA. Pooh—that's not philosophy, that's common sense.

CYNTHIA. Growing old's not like I expected it to be. I thought one *would* feel different and that would somehow make things seem right. But one feels just the same.

DORA. Oh, yes—I think everyone notices that. (*She stops making water-lilies.*)

CYNTHIA. Do you mean one always feels it, even till——

DORA. Till the very end, I expect. I've always felt exactly the same. And I've always felt a little surprised that age could happen to me—and a little unbelieving. I've sometimes wondered——

CYNTHIA. Go on, Mother.

DORA. I've never put it into words before. But I have wondered if that might be—an evidence of immortality; if one's real, true self might always be young, perfect and immutable.

CYNTHIA. Do you mean the soul?

DORA. I don't know why, but I've never liked the word "soul." When I was a child I always imagined the soul was a bit of brown fog. I've never quite been able to get over it. I prefer to think of one's *real* self, the self no one else ever quite knows. Can you ever quite believe that you'll die?

CYNTHIA. No. One knows one must—but one doesn't believe it.

DORA. That's your real self. It knows something about immortality. And I think it knows something about youth. I'm more and more convinced that nothing lovely can ever be quite lost.

CYNTHIA. I wonder if that would link up with modern time theories?

DORA. I never could make head nor tail of those. But it's all in the Bible—" That which hath been is now ; and that which is to be hath already been; and God requireth that which is past." There isn't much you can teach the writer of Ecclesiastes.

CYNTHIA. "And God requireth that which is past." (*She puts her hand on her mother's.*) Thank you, darling.

DORA. Cynthia, dear—I've been trying to talk to you all this week-end. You're not happy.

CYNTHIA (*desperately*). Yes, I am, Mother—perfectly happy.

DORA. But anyone can see you're not. Of course, your father and I have realized for years that there are things in your life you don't want us to know about and we should never dream of trying to force your confidence. But don't stay away another seven years—because it really isn't necessary.

CYNTHIA. Mother, you're just imagining things.

DORA. Nonsense, dear.

CYNTHIA (*looking out front*). Did Edna tell you ?

DORA. I shouldn't dream of gossiping about you with Edna.

(CYNTHIA *looks gratefully at* DORA.)

But I do know that no woman of your temperament who doesn't marry could have spent all those years in Paris in—well, shall we say, a strictly conventional manner.

CYNTHIA. Don't you mind ?

DORA. I can't think anything you could do quite terrible enough to make me want to lose touch with you.

CYNTHIA. It wasn't very terrible. We'd have been married if we could have been.

DORA. Was he French ?

CYNTHIA. No—English. His wife is French.

DORA. She won't divorce him ?

CYNTHIA. No. It's over, Mother. He went back to her. I expect he got tired of me.

DORA. My dearest child.

CYNTHIA. Oh, I'm all right. It knocked me out for a bit, but I'm over it now——

DORA. And is this all that's kept you away from us for seven years ?

CYNTHIA. I suppose so. Mother, how you've changed. You used to be so strict in your ideas.

DORA. I had four young daughters to bring up. But I *have* changed. There wouldn't be much point in living to be seventy if one didn't.

CYNTHIA (*laying her hand on* DORA). I always did like you better than any woman I ever met.

DORA. My dear !—Must you—must you go back to Paris ?

CYNTHIA (*letting go of* DORA). I've finished with Paris. I can go to Raquelle's London house if I like ; or I think she'd send me to America.

DORA. Why not come home for a little while, dear ?

CYNTHIA. You mean just stay on ?

DORA. Only for a short time, of course—we'd never try to keep you. But just for a little holiday—you used to be so fond of the autumn—and we could slip up to town for some theatres and concerts ; do you remember our little jaunts ? And if you could stay till spring, it's so very beautiful here. The spring never gets any older, you know. (*She smiles tentatively at*

CYNTHIA, *who has turned away, then pulls herself up.*)   Very well,
my dear, I won't press it, of course.   I just thought you might
like it.
     CYNTHIA.   I think I'd like it more than anything in the world.
     DORA.   You mean you'll stay ?
     CYNTHIA (*rising to behind* DORA'S *chair*).   If you really fancy
an elderly prodigal daughter.   (*She goes to kiss* DORA.)   Darling
—you're trembling, and you sounded so calm.
     DORA.   I was just a little nervous.
     CYNTHIA.   Oh, Mother——
     DORA.   Good gracious, don't start to cry or you'll simply
wreck your face.   Now hurry up and dress.

(FENNY, *in evening dress, enters* R.   CYNTHIA *turns away and
                     exits.*)

I'll come with you and get you a glass of sherry.   Fenny, would
you do the water-lilies ?   I'm afraid I wasn't quite concentrating
on them.

(DORA *goes out into the hall.*   FENNY *starts to fold "* water-lilies.*"
     NICHOLAS *is heard calling, "* Fenny.*"   For a moment she thinks
     of escaping, but he enters from the hall.*)

     NICHOLAS.   Oh !   There you are.   I took a telephone message
for you—about half an hour ago.   I couldn't find you anywhere.
(*He comes down* L. *to behind* CHARLES'S *chair.*)
     FENNY.   I was dressing.
     NICHOLAS.   Your charming chicken-farming friend wants you
to take tea with him to-morrow at four-thirty.   At his delightful
bungalow so appropriately called " The Nest."
     FENNY.   Thank you.
     NICHOLAS.   Shall you go ?
     FENNY.   If I can be spared.   It'll be quiet when you've all
gone.   Yes, I think I shall go.
     NICHOLAS.   What fun !   You have such good taste in men.
(*He goes up towards the door, then turns to* FENNY.)
     FENNY.   Is that meant to be rude ?
     NICHOLAS.   Yes, I think it is.   (*He comes down to* FENNY.)
Good lord, what's the matter with you, Fenny ?
     FENNY.   What do you mean ?
     NICHOLAS.   Encouraging this poor wretched man.   Before
you know where you are he'll be proposing to you.
     FENNY.   Is that a crime ?
     NICHOLAS.   Oh—perhaps he's proposed already ?   My God,
I believe he has.   Are you going to accept him ?
     FENNY.   I haven't made up my mind.
     NICHOLAS.   You're not serious ?
     FENNY.   Certainly I am.   And it's none of your business.
     NICHOLAS.   It's the business of the whole family—we've

known and liked you for ten years.   The man's a common little
bounder.

FENNY.   I don't think so.

NICHOLAS.   I suppose you were playing Kenneth off against
him last night to bring him up to the scratch.   I can't think
why you left me out—I should have been delighted to have
helped.   Good lord, I couldn't have believed you'd make yourself so cheap.

FENNY.   Please go away.

NICHOLAS.   Dressing yourself up and giggling and flirting.
(*He goes up to the fire.*)   And if you're going to use rouge you'd
better learn to use it properly.

FENNY.   I'm not using rouge.

NICHOLAS.   You were last night.   If you want to know, you
looked like an elderly schoolgirl.   (*He comes down to* FENNY.)
What a damnable thing to say.   I'm sorry, Fenny.

(FENNY *bends over the napkin-folding.*)

It wasn't true, anyhow.   You looked very pretty.   I've hurt you,
haven't I ?   Do you remember wondering if I could be cruel ?

FENNY.   You said you never could be to me.   (*She finishes
a napkin and puts it in* NICHOLAS's *place.*)

NICHOLAS.   Listen, my dear.   There must be something
behind this that I don't understand.

(FENNY *takes up another napkin and crumples it.*)

Are you thinking of marriage as a safeguard for the future ?

FENNY.   It's got nothing to do with that.

NICHOLAS.   Then what the devil is it ?   Good lord, I believe
Edna was right.

FENNY (*frantic—facing him*).   What do you mean ?

NICHOLAS.   She said once that most women would rather
marry anyone than no one.

FENNY.   I haven't made up my mind to marry him.

NICHOLAS.   I can't conceive how you could even let him
propose.   Oh lord, let's chuck it or I shall be rude again.   Somehow the very thought of it makes my blood boil.   (*He goes to*
CHARLES's *place, turns the chair towards the audience and sits.*)
Sorry I've been so insulting.

FENNY.   That's all right.   (*She finds the crumpled napkin in
her hand.*)   Are you going to do Grand Toast to-night ?

NICHOLAS.   I suppose so.   I never felt less like it.   Funny,
that, I usually rather enjoy it.   I'd better walk round the garden
and try to mug something up.   (*Rising to behind the chair.*)
You're making an awful mess of those napkins.

FENNY.   You've been a little distracting.

NICHOLAS.   Poor old Fenny.   You will marry him, of course
—otherwise you'd never have led him on.   Well, you must see

something in him. God, I couldn't be more disappointed in anyone.

(*He goes out to the hall.* FENNY *sits and buries her face in her hands. After a second* CHARLES *comes from the* R., *carrying four champagne bottles.*)

CHARLES. Got a headache, my dear ?
FENNY (*jumping up and coming round* R. *end of the table to below it,* R.C.). Just a bit. It'll go off.

(CHARLES *puts the bottles down, then goes to her and puts his hand on her shoulder.*)

CHARLES. What is it, Fenny ?
FENNY (*bursting into tears*). Oh, I can't bear it any longer. Couldn't I say I was ill ? All this long evening——
CHARLES. Fenny—our Golden Wedding evening ?
FENNY. I'm sorry. But I can't stand any more. How could he ? How could he ?
CHARLES. Nicholas, of course.
FENNY. Oh, everyone knows.
CHARLES. *He* certainly doesn't.
FENNY. No. That's the one bit of comfort there is. Mr. Randolph, please tell me—was I vulgar and silly last night ?
CHARLES. You were a little skittish.
FENNY. He was so cruel.
CHARLES. Cruel ?
FENNY. But it's not his fault. Don't you see, he was so disappointed in me. And I've got to go on pretending to be what he thinks I am now—never to let him see——
CHARLES. Why ?
FENNY. Pride, I suppose.
CHARLES. Oh, I see. Is pride worth all that trouble ? I never had any myself, of course. Now pull yourself together, my dear. (*He pats her and goes away to above the table and puts two chairs in place.*) If you really want to go to bed you'd better go at once and I'll make your excuses.
FENNY. No, I couldn't—not your Golden Wedding dinner. I'll be all right. (*Going up towards the door* R.) I'll go and do my face.
CHARLES. Was Nicholas really unkind ?
FENNY. Terribly—and he's always been so sweet to me.
CHARLES (*thoughtfully*). Yes, I know.
FENNY. Do you think I *could* marry Mr. Jones ?
CHARLES. Mr. Jones ?
FENNY. You know—at the chicken farm.
CHARLES. Good gracious ! I should hardly have said so.
FENNY. I don't think so either. I don't even like hens.

(*She rushes out* ʀ. Cʜᴀʀʟᴇꜱ *is extremely thoughtful.* Dᴏʀᴀ *enters from the hall. She comes down* ʟ., *then right across in front of the table to* ʀ.ᴄ. Cʜᴀʀʟᴇꜱ *goes to her.*)

Dᴏʀᴀ. Oh, there you are. My dear, it's all right.

Cʜᴀʀʟᴇꜱ. What is ?

Dᴏʀᴀ. Cynthia. I had it out with her. And really it's nothing terrible—well, of course, it is, but times change. Anyhow, it's over—and she's staying on indefinitely—and she'll be able to help me with Scrap as her father's marrying again——

Cʜᴀʀʟᴇꜱ. Here, hold hard.

Dᴏʀᴀ. I'd a letter from him yesterday—I told you—didn't I ? Well, I meant to. He wants us to take sole charge for the time being and she's taken a tremendous fancy to Cynthia. Oh dear——

Cʜᴀʀʟᴇꜱ. What ?

Dᴏʀᴀ (*pointing up at a portrait on the wall* ʀ.). I was thinking how terribly shocked my dear mother would have been about Cynthia. She had such rigid principles.

Cʜᴀʀʟᴇꜱ (*turning and looking at the picture*). Yes.

Dᴏʀᴀ (*moving up to above* Cʜᴀʀʟᴇꜱ). But it's better to lose a principle than lose a daughter. I've had three glasses of sherry. (*She sits in a chair above the table.*)

Cʜᴀʀʟᴇꜱ (*laughing*). Dora !

Dᴏʀᴀ. With Cynthia, just to cheer her up.

(Hᴜɢʜ *and* Lᴀᴜʀᴇʟ, *dressed for dinner and looking very handsome, come in from the hall.* Hᴜɢʜ *comes down to* Cʜᴀʀʟᴇꜱ's *chair and sits.*)

Lᴀᴜʀᴇʟ. Can we help ?

Hᴜɢʜ. Grannie, you look ravishing.

Lᴀᴜʀᴇʟ (*coming along the table to* ʟ. *of* Dᴏʀᴀ). Oh, I do wish baby was old enough to come to this dinner.

(Cʜᴀʀʟᴇꜱ *goes to the sideboard.*)

Dᴏʀᴀ. I was wondering if you'd like to borrow Nanny for a few months. You've got room for her.

Lᴀᴜʀᴇʟ. You don't mean it ? How marvellous !

Hᴜɢʜ. Fancy you planning that out.

Dᴏʀᴀ. As a matter of fact, I've just this second thought of it. And your grandfather will give you a pound a week for her keep, won't you, dear ?

Cʜᴀʀʟᴇꜱ. Yes, dear. (*Going to* Dᴏʀᴀ.) Are you quite all right ?

Dᴏʀᴀ. Quite. (*She has been wildly folding napkins and now surveys them.*) But there won't be any water-lilies. We'll have some nice, simple cocked hats. (*She rises.*)

(GERTRUDE *enters* R. *with spirit lamps for hotplate.* CHARLES *takes them from her and puts them under the hotplate on the sideboard.*)

Bring some more napkins, Gertrude.

GERTRUDE. *More* napkins, madam ?

DORA. Certainly. Something has occurred to these.

(GERTRUDE *goes out* R. HUGH *rises to behind the chair.*)

(CHARLES *goes to the door up* R.)

Where are you going ?

CHARLES. I just want to have a word with Nicholas.

DORA. Ring the dressing gong, will you, dear ?

(CHARLES *goes out* R., *shutting the door.*)

LAUREL. I simply can't believe it about Nanny. You are the kindest people.

DORA (*crossing behind* LAUREL *to* L. *end of the table*). Well, I do think we're rather a pleasant family ; (*she looks into a mustard-pot*) and I'm sure God has been very good to us and I thank Him with all my heart.

(GERTRUDE *enters with fresh napkins, which she puts on the sideboard.*)

Gertrude, this mustard isn't fresh—tell Annie to make some more and be quick about it.

The gong booms as—

The CURTAIN *falls.*

SCENE 2

SCENE.—*The Dining-room.*
     The lamps have been put out and the table, lit by the silver candelabra, is a pool of light in the dark room. The entire family and FENNY *are seated round it. Dinner is finished. There is laughter and talk.* CHARLES *and* EDNA *are smoking.*

CHARLES. Now then, Nicholas——
BILL. Come on, Uncle Nick.
DORA. Ssh, everyone.

(NICHOLAS *rises.* HUGH, LAUREL *and the children applaud.* NICHOLAS *stands* R. *of his chair.* HILDA, LAUREL *and* EDNA *turn their chairs slightly to* R. BILL *leans right forward.* SCRAP *and* CYNTHIA, *their arms round each other, lean forward.*)

NICHOLAS. We are an abstemious family, both in drink and
speeches. We make one speech and drink one family toast—
at Christmas, at New Year and at all our family gatherings. So
we have always done, right back, I believe, into Great-grandfather's day. But to-night, wondering what I should say to
you, it seemed to me another toast was called for. None of my
generation remembers a Golden Wedding in this house and,
indeed, I think they are rarer throughout the world, in these days
of later marriage and earlier divorce.

(*Laugh from the table.*)

It is a great occasion for us all, and one, I felt, which could well
warrant a break with our tradition. And so I planned a separate
toast for Father and Mother on their Golden Wedding day.

(*There is a murmur of applause, but* NICHOLAS *quells it.*)

And then I knew this could not be. For they *are* the family
and never, for any occasion, shall they be separated from it in
our thoughts. We have already given them our presents, good
wishes and our love, which, indeed, is always theirs, and now
this Golden Wedding is no longer theirs alone, but ours to share
with them. And so, once more I shall propose Grand Toast to
our family.

(*Approval from the table, which swells up and dies.*)

CHARLES⎱ (*together*). ⎰Quite right.
HUGH ⎰   ⎱Hear, hear.
NICHOLAS. Wandering round the garden just now, I was
trying to remember when I first proposed this toast——
DORA. The year your father had laryngitis, dear.
HILDA. Nineteen-nineteen.
DORA. Oh no, Hilda——
CHARLES. Ssh, you two.
NICHOLAS. Whatever the year, I know I felt very young and
nervous. I had mugged up three quotations and two funny
stories which I meant to tell with exquisite point ; and when the
moment came, I didn't use any of them.

(*Slight laugh from the table.*)

Perhaps the patron saint of family gatherings came to my aid.
If so, I hope he may come again to-night. For again, nothing
that I planned seems quite right. I haven't even a quotation
and I couldn't make a joke to save my life. For it came to me
suddenly just now that a family gathering like this is no joking
matter. One hears so many jokes against families, of family
quarrels, family jealousies, family tyrannies. Always the family
is either the villain or the clown of the piece. Well, the clown
shall stand, for clowns are likeable folk ; but not the villain.

And, for me at least, to-night it shall play the hero. And it does
possess heroic qualities. How else has it survived ? It no
longer has the power of the tyrant. Who to-day ever feels any
real family authority ? Even the children do exactly what they
like——

BILL. Ooh, not quite, Uncle Nick.

(*Slight laughter.* FLOUNCY *nudges* BILL.)

NICHOLAS. Near enough, young Bill—look at you, interrupting your aged uncle's touching speech—no reverence, no
awe. But I bet you'll make as good a family man as any of
us.

(*Laugh from the table.*)

We grumble at our families, we treat them as a bad joke, we hear
on every hand that family ties are slackening—and yet, we pack
the trains at Christmas going home.

(CHARLES *nods approvingly.*)

NICHOLAS. A sense of duty only ? I wonder. (*Slight pause.*)
We are a very ordinary family. We own no crests, no heirlooms,
and our few ancestors are very badly painted.

(*Slight laugh from the table.*)

I wonder what they would think of us, Great-grandfather with
his twinkle and Grandmamma, who wasn't quite as fierce as that.
(*He looks up at the portrait.*)

(*Slight laugh from the table.*)

But she *was* a little fierce. I think she might shake her head and
say, " The family isn't what it was." And there, most honoured
Grandmamma, lies its strength. It is, like nearly every British
institution, adaptable. It bends, it stretches—but it never
breaks. And so I give you our toast. From that young man
upstairs who has had the impudence to make me a great-uncle—

(*Murmur from* LAUREL *and* HUGH.)

—to Mother and Father on their Golden Wedding ; through four
generations of us ; and to those who have gone, and those who
are to come. To the family—that dear octopus from whose
tentacles we never quite escape nor, in our inmost hearts, ever
quite wish to. Ladies and gentlemen, Grand Toast.

(*The family rise and raise their glasses.*)

ALL. Grand Toast.

(*The toast is drunk ; then laughter and conversation break out.*)

CYNTHIA⎱ (*together*).   ⎰Bravo, Nicholas.
CHARLES⎰   ⎱Very good indeed, my boy.

(All sit.)

BILL.   Not one funny story.

EDNA.   I never heard you so emotional, Nicholas.

CYNTHIA.   We liked it, didn't we, Scrap ?

CHARLES.   I rather query one of your similes——

DORA.   Discuss it in the drawing-room, will you, dear ? Gertrude'll be on the rampage. Good gracious, we never said after-dinner grace. Charles dear——

CHARLES.   Yes, my love.

(He rises and the others follow suit.)

For these and all Thy blessings, we thank Thee, Lord.

*(Various members of the family say " Amen."   MARGERY pinches
    BILL.)*

BILL.   You needn't pinch me, Mummie, I wasn't going to.

DORA.   Get the maids started, Fenny.

*(The family go out into the hall, laughing and talking and chaffing
NICHOLAS about his speech.   KENNETH comes round and moves
DORA's chair out for her.   EDNA goes up stage behind her chair.
LAUREL joins EDNA.   HILDA and FENNY go towards the doors.
HUGH and CHARLES open the doors.   BELLE goes to CHARLES.
MARGERY collects BILL and FLOUNCY each side of her.   CYNTHIA
and SCRAP come along in front of the table, arms round each other.
DORA kisses NICHOLAS and crosses and exits first.   She is
followed by HILDA and BELLE ; MARGERY, BILL and FLOUNCY ;
EDNA, LAUREL and HUGH ; KENNETH and NICHOLAS ;
CYNTHIA and SCRAP and CHARLES.   NICHOLAS and KENNETH
close the doors.   Voices emerge from the general talk.)*

BELLE.   I think you should have replied, Charles.

CHARLES.   No, no—one speech is enough.

KENNETH.   All you want to do now, old man, is to start a
family for yourself.

*(The doors close on the party and the voices dwindle.   FENNY is
alone on the stage.   She stands leaning against the mantelpiece.
She looks round the table and sees that CHARLES has left his glasses.
She crosses to the sideboard and lights the lamp, then goes below
the table and starts to stack the plates.*

NICHOLAS *enters suddenly.)*

FENNY *(with false brightness)*.   Hello.

NICHOLAS.   Father forgot his glasses.

FENNY *(pointing to L. end of the table)*.   They're there.

NICHOLAS.   Still angry with me ?

FENNY.   You were the angry one.

NICHOLAS.   Shall we make it up ?

FENNY.   If you like. It doesn't matter, anyhow.

NICHOLAS (*going to* FENNY). It matters to me. Friends?

FENNY. Of course. (*She looks up, reading his eyes.*) You know, don't you?

NICHOLAS. Yes.

FENNY. Did Edna tell you?

NICHOLAS. No.

FENNY. Who did, then?—Oh, I know—your father.

(NICHOLAS *nods.*)

He said pride wasn't important. Yes, he was right. I think I'm rather glad you know. How queer! I used to think it would be the end of the world. You don't mind terribly, do you? It needn't worry you or embarrass you. After to-night we'll never refer to it again.

NICHOLAS. Will you marry me, Fenny?

FENNY (*recoiling*). No! Oh, how could you? I can't help loving you, I'm not ashamed of it, it's been my secret happiness for years. But to say that to me when I know it's meaningless! I'm sorry. I expect you meant to be kind. But pity can be very humiliating.

NICHOLAS. Don't be a juggins, dear—men don't propose out of pity.

FENNY. Do you mean you're in love with me?

NICHOLAS. I really love you, Fenny. You don't believe me?

FENNY. I don't know. You *are* a truthful person. But surely you couldn't find that out suddenly, just because your father told you, just in an hour or two.

NICHOLAS. Almost in a flash. Listen; I believe I've been in love with you for years and never realized it. And then, after we'd been sitting by the fire the other evening, something Edna said—quite inadvertently—made me see you as a different person. Do you remember in the nursery, Fenny, you on the cupboard?

FENNY. Yes.

NICHOLAS. I think I almost knew I loved you then. But last night—you and your goings-on with Kenneth and that wretched chicken farmer—I thought Edna must have been talking through her hat. I could cheerfully have killed the lot of you. I'm very much ashamed of myself. I suppose I was just plain jealous.

FENNY. How glorious!

NICHOLAS. What loathsome things I said to you. You'll never see a worse side of me than you've seen this week-end. The teething stage of love is very confusing.

FENNY. Nicholas, was that speech you made just now sincere? You've never made a speech like that before.

NICHOLAS. I couldn't have done, never in my life. That speech was not only to the family, but to our future.

(He takes her in his arms and kisses her. BILL *enters from the hall.)*

BILL. Swelp me!

(They break away from each other.)

NICHOLAS. Bill, Fenny's going to marry me.

BILL. Crickey, I am pleased. *(Turning up to the door.)* That beastly Flouncy's not going to tell this one.

(He rushes out.)

FENNY. No, wait—not yet——

NICHOLAS. My dear, you'll never muzzle that.

BILL *(off stage).* Listen—listen, everyone—Nicholas and Fenny are engaged——

(There is a murmur of voices, questions, and general excitement.)

NICHOLAS. Are you ready ? *(He gives* FENNY *a quick kiss.)* Come on.

He puts his arm round her and marches her towards the door as—

The CURTAIN *falls.*

ACT III, SCENE 1

ACT III, SCENE 2

PROPERTY PLOT

ACT I

Writing-desk down R.
 On it.—Blotter, inkstand with pen and pencil, writing-paper, envelopes, leather case for papers, small lamp.
Waste-paper basket under desk down R.
 In it.—Gold and pink telegram envelopes, paper, etc.
Elbow chair L. of desk.
Table above door R.
 On it.—Wooden box.
Chair above table up R.
Tallboy above chair up R.
 On it.—Lamp, ashtray.
 In it.—Books : one practical on third shelf up, downstage section ; one practical on second shelf up, downstage section.
Barometer on wall below tallboy.
Grandfather clock L. of dining-room doors up R.C.
Stair carpet.
Pedestal lamp L. of clock, on stairs.
Circular table R. of staircase.
 On it.—2 leather-bound books.
Chest up L. above sofa.
 On it.—Chinese bowl.
Carpet runner up stage of sofa.
Green curtain with rod, on kitchen door L.
Sofa R. of fireplace.
 On it.—Modern book (indicator), 3 cushions.
Standard lamp L. of sofa.
Occasional table L. of settee.
 On it.—Vase of flowers, spectacles in case, clock (to be facing R.), photo in silver frame to face front.
Mantelpiece.
 On it.—Pair of Dresden candlesticks, pair of Dresden figures, Dresden group, 2 ornate snuff-boxes.
Painting over fireplace (Peter).
Fender and fireirons. Hearth-brush to be downstage end.
Bellows to lean upstage end of fireplace.
2 logs downstage end of grate.
Firestool R. of fender.
Rug R. of fireplace.
Brass coal-box below fireplace.
 On it.—Coal-glove.
Canterbury down stage of coal box.
 In it.—Magazines, " Tatler," " Sketch," etc., " Times," " Telegraph."
Armchair down stage of coal-box—facing up R.
 On it.—Cushion.
Secretaire down L.
 In it.—9 china pieces.
Large elbow chair L.C., facing L.
Large green carpet C.

Drumhead table R.C.

On it.—Ashtray, silver cigarette-box with cigarettes, silver match-box, pile of telegrams (cable to be second in pile), paper-weight on top, silver salver with visiting-cards on it, dead roses in bowl, one fresh rose to be upstage end.

In drawer R. of table.—Check duster.

Set up L. in dining-room, CHARLES's chair (elbow chair from Act III set).

Boot-scraper outside door down R.

Mat outside door down R.

Pictures.—4 on staircase wall.

2 French prints on wall R. of double doors.

1 large print down L.

1 small print down L.

Oil painting (portrait) on dining-room backing.

Carpet, recess of dining-room doors up R.

Pair of curtains and pelmet over window down R. (closed).

Pair of curtains and pelmet over window above door R. (closed).

Off R.

Chrysanthemums, pair of garden scissors, torch (FENNY).

Suitcase (NICHOLAS).

In it.—Box of paints (wrapped), 3 small leather-bound books, small parcel (wrapped), book (wrapped), posy of flowers in box, jeweller's case (unwrapped), brooch, sponge-bag, tail-coat, white tie, dress-shirt, collars, brushes, pair of shoes, slippers, tweed coat, etc.

Personal Properties.

Cigarette-case, matches (NICHOLAS).

Cigar (small) (CHARLES).

Cigar (small) (KENNETH).

Cigarette-case, matches (EDNA).

Gloves and handbag (BELLE).

Diary (NICHOLAS).

Goloshes (FLOUNCY).

Cigarette (HUGH).

Notebook and Pencil (HILDA).

White dress (FENNY).

2 overcoats (HUGH and LAUREL).

Off L.

Thin bar of chocolate (BILL).

Mahogany tray (NICHOLAS).

On it.—4 small plates, 1 plate sardine sandwiches, 1 plate potted meat sandwiches.

Lacquer tray (FENNY).

On it.—3 cups, saucers and spoons, jug of cocoa, sugar-basin.

Silver tray (MARGERY).

On it.—6 glasses, syphon in silver holder, decanter of whisky.

Large box of chocolates (BILL).

Money (coins) (HILDA).

6 rubber hot-water bottles (3 in covers) (GERTRUDE).

1 stone hot-water bottle (GERTRUDE).

Coal-glove (re-set after exit of EDNA) (EDNA).

White dress (FENNY).

Hugh and Laurel's overcoats (LAUREL).

Effects.

Clock-strike (chime) eleven o'clock (grandfather clock).

Crackle of burning wood.

ACT II

Scene 1.

Nursing-chair down R. facing L.
  On it.—Cushion.
Fireguard (large).
  In it.—Poker upstage end.
Toasting-fork on wall L. of fire.
Easy chair L. of fireguard.
  On it.—Cushion, paint-box (with three brushes, also one short one for
gold paint). Cupboard up R. above fire.
  In it.—Games of Ludo, Halma, Snakes and Ladders ; one-armed teddy-
bear, cup with handle off, various boxes, scraps and transfers to
be stuck on inside of doors, toys, etc.
  On it.—Empty cracker-box.
Overmantel over fire.
  On it.—Box of matches, money-box, 2 china mugs, china jug, toy animals,
etc.
Small step-ladder leaning against wall above cupboard.
Window-seat with squab seat.
  In it.—6 magazines—including fashion paper, " Country Life " and
" Riding."
Pair of red curtains at window on pole.
Rocking-horse up L.C. between window and door.
Bookcase shelves up L. between doors.
  On them.—Blackberry-basket, books (children's), box of coloured chalks,
pencil-boxes, old paint-box, old chocolate-box, filled with oddments,
string, etc., train and lines.
  Under them.—Child's fort.
Upright piano down L. below downstage door (lid closed).
  On it.—6-photo frame folder, tumbler with rose, 3 loose petals.
Piano-stool R. of piano.
Carpet C.
Table L.C.
  On it.—White cloth.
    Tray. *On it.*—Teapot, hot-water jug ($\frac{1}{4}$ full), milk-jug, plate-knife,
cup and saucer, NANNY's serviette (opened) and ring. Sugar-basin,
loaf and knife on platter, cruet, marmalade-pot and spoon, butter-
dish with butter, 3 plates and knives, 3 mugs (one bluebird), 3
serviettes (opened) and rings.
Chair R. of table.
Chair above table.
2 chairs L. of table.
Speaking-tube down R. above lift (whistle).
Baby's high chair down L. below piano.
Set piano down L. (off stage).
Set piano understage.
Carpet down stage of backing to landing door.
Rag mat R.C. front of fire.
Centre section of window open at top.
Pictures.—1 down R. over lift.
    1 over rocking-horse.
    1 above doors on backing L.C.
    2 on wall up L. on landing.
    1 over bookshelves up L.
    1 down stage of door down L.
    2 over piano.
    1 on nursery backing.

During scene : Strike props from lift and set props for Scene 2.

Off L.
Plate of cakes (CYNTHIA).
12 dance programmes (MARGERY).
Book (novel) (HILDA).
Blackberry-basket with about 20 blackberries, reset (BILL).

Effect.
Lift descending.

SCENE 2

Strike.
Small step-ladder from up R.
Paint-box, cup, magazines from table L.C.
Book from easy chair L. of fire.
Plate of cakes, dance programmes from table L.C.
Blackberry-basket.
Chair above piano (moved from L. of table during Scene 1) to be left
   as set for Act II, Scenes 2 and 3.

Re-set.
Easy chair L. of fireguard to fireguard.
Table L.C. to new mark 6 inches to L.
Three chairs at table L.C. to be pushed under it.
Piano lid open.
Piano stool pulled out. Seat must revolve.

Set.
White dress (used in Act I) on easy chair L. of fire.
Needle, threaded with white cotton in dress.
Small work-basket on floor down R. of easy chair L. of fire.
   In it.—Wools, cottons, needles, thimble, etc.
Scissors and reel of white cotton on mantelpiece.
Box of matches on mantelpiece.
Green tablecloth on table L.C.
Jigsaw puzzle (partly done) on drawing board, on L. end of table L.C.
2 large dishes of crumpets (with covers) on bottom shelf of service lift
   (set during Act II, Scene 1).
Chocolate cake (prop.) on plate on top shelf of service lift (set during
   Act II, Scene 1).
Centre section of window closed, but not catched.

Off L.
Bottle of hand lotion (wrapped) (NICHOLAS).
Oil-lamp (NANNY).
Silver tray (GERTRUDE).
   On it.—Silver teapot, silver hot-water jug, silver milk-jug, silver
   sugar-basin and tongs, 4 cups and saucers (set ready) with spoons,
   4 plates.
Mahogany tray (NANNY).
   On it.—3 cups and saucers, 4 plates (stacked), 3 spoons, salt-cellar
   and spoon, china slop-basin, cake (prop.), 3 mugs.

Effects.
Whistle for service lift.
Clock strike (stable), five o'clock.

SCENE 3

Strike.
Scissors and reel of cotton from overmantel.
Jigsaw puzzle from under rocking-horse.

Trays of tea-things from table **L. C.**
Bottle of hand lotion.

Re-set.

Easy chair **L.** of fire to opening mark, Scene 1.
Table **L.C.** re-set on Scene 2 marks.
3 chairs at table **L.C.** pushed under as in Scene 2.
Work-basket from cupboard up **R.** to table **L.C.** (see " Set ").
Close lift panel.
Close piano.

Set.

Work-basket upstage **L.** end of table **L.C.**
Baby's dress, with blue ribbon and bodkin, threaded, on work-basket.
Coal-scuttle below fireguard down **R.**, with coal.
Coal-glove on coal.
Fireguard (small) inside large fender.

Off **L.**

Dance programme (KENNETH).
Child's book (" Alice in Wonderland ") (CYNTHIA).

Effect.

Clock-strike (stable), twelve o'clock.

ACT III

SCENE 1

Chair down **R.**
Sideboard up stage of chair.
    On it.—Jar of salted almonds, box of chocolates, 2 silver boat trays for
        chocolates, box of matches, oil-lamp, jug of water, hotplate stand.
    In downstage cupboard of sideboard.—2 cruets (with practically no
        mustard)—cruets must be on bottom shelf—sugar-shaker, silver
        toast-rack.
Cupboard up **R.**
    In it.—*Top shelf :* 18 cut-glass tumblers, 6 champagne glasses, 6 port
        glasses.
        Middle shelf : 18 fruit-plates, 4 coloured plates, 2 Victorian vases,
            china teapot, toast-rack, inkstand.
        Bottom shelf : china jug, china vase, decanter, 3 glass vases.
        Bottom of cupboard : epergne, cheese-dish with lid, three-division
            cheese-dish, glass vase, decanter.
Fender.
Fireirons.
Chair up **R.**, **R.** of cupboard.
Chair **R.** of fire.
Chair **L.** of fire.
Picture over fire (Great-grandfather).
3 bronze figures on mantelpiece.
2 3-branch candelabra (practical) on mantelpiece.
2 chairs up **L.**, front of upstage window.
2 chairs down **L.**, front of downstage window.
Chair down **L.**
Pair of curtains on window up **L.** closed.
Pair of curtains on window down **L.** closed.
Picture down **R.** above sideboard (Grandmamma).
Large elbow chair **L.** of dining-table (set out).
Elbow chair **R.** of dining-table (set out).
Carpet **C.**
Small runner down stage of double doors.

Table up L. (between windows).
  On it.—Oil-lamp.
Small runner down stage of cupboard.
Dining-table c.
  On it.—Cut-glass bowl of asters, on lace mat, with grid (centre of table),
    2 cut-glass dishes (either side of bowl).

(Dinner is being laid for fifteen people, eleven places have been laid and
  four partly. The following plot reads from stage R. to L.)

Extreme R. of Table.
  * *Place fully laid* with large knife, small knife, dessert spoon and fork,
    soup spoon, large fork, fish knife and fork, champagne glass, port-
    wine glass, cork mat, lace mat.

Upstage side of Table (moving Stage R. to L.).
  Next 5 places fully laid as above, *.
  Next 2 places partly laid as follows : Cork mat, lace mat, large knife,
    small knife, champagne glass, port-wine glass.

Extreme L. of Table.
  Cork mat, lace mat, large knife, small knife, champagne glass, port-wine
    glass.

In front of above place.
  Large cork mat, carving-knive and fork, 2 rests.

Downstage side of Table (R. to L.).
  2 places fully laid, refer to *.
  Next 3 places fully laid—but without glasses. (Children's places.)
  Last place partly laid with cork mat, lace mat, large knife, small knife,
    champagne glass, port-wine glass.
Glass cloth (polisher) on R. upstage corner of table.
Cutlery basket on L. downstage corner of table.
  In it.—9 large forks, 10 dessert spoons and forks, 9 fish knives and
    forks, 9 soup spoons, knife-sharpener.
Oil painting (Grandmamma) over sideboard.
Oil painting down R.
Oil painting over door R.
Plaque over cupboard R.C.
Oil painting (Great-grandfather) over fireplace,
3 plates over double doors.
2 oil paintings up stage of chair down L.
Oil painting above chair down L.

3 oil paintings on hall backing.

  Set up L. above double doors.
  Green curtains and pelmet.
  Kidney-shaped desk and chair (as Act 1),
  Drumhead table (as Act I), R. of desk.
  Round table R. of double doors.
  Carpet from Act I.

Off up L.
  Orchids in chip basket (NANNY).

Off R.
  9 napkins (folded) (GERTRUDE).
  4 champagne bottles (full) (CHARLES).
  2 spirit lamps (GERTRUDE).
  6 napkins (folded) (GERTRUDE).
  (Set ready—15 napkins (used) off stage, each member of the cast will
    take a napkin on for Scene 2.)

SCENE 2

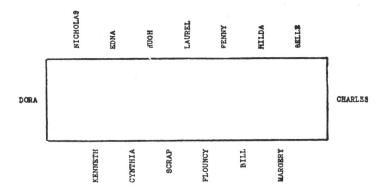

Plan showing positions at table, Act III, Scene 2.

Effect.
    Gong, off R.

Strike.
    All knives, forks, spoons, carving-knife, carving-fork and rests, cork mats, lace mats, half the almonds in dishes, half the chocolates in boat trays, napkins, cruets—from dining-table.
    15 dessert plates, 3 full champagne bottles, epergne and napkins—from sideboard.
    2 candelabra from mantelpiece.

Set.
    15 dessert plates, 15 dessert knives and forks, 15 lace mats, 15 finger-bowls. (A dessert plate, lace mat, knife and fork, finger-bowl in each place. Dessert plates to have peelings on them, apple-peel, banana-skins, etc.)
    Spectacles in case—extreme L. end of table.
    2 candelabra (electric), 2 bowls of fruit (with bananas, apples, oranges, grapes and nuts).
    Port to be poured in 3 port glasses only (last glass R. end above table, last glass R. end below table, and glass extreme L. end of table.)
    Champagne to be poured in all remaining champagne glasses on table.
    7 chairs above table (re-set one from above sideboard, 1 from cupboard, 2 from fireplace, 2 from window up L., 2 from window down L. These chairs have been raised 2 inches higher and must be above table.) 6 chairs below table (one from down R., one from down L. and one dining-chair and 3 nursery chairs (Act II) brought on).
    4 small candles (electric), c. table.
    3 empty champagne bottles—on sideboard.

Personal Properties.
    Cigarette (EDNA).
    Cigar (CHARLES).

Printed in Great Britain by
Billing & Sons Ltd, Worcester